The Vegan Keto Cookbook

Top 100 Delicious Vegan Ketogenic Recipes For Healthy Living

AMY ZACKARY

Copyright © 2018 Amy Zackary

All rights reserved. No part of this publication may be reproduced, distributed, or transmitted in any form or by any means, including photocopying, recording, or other electronic or mechanical methods, without the prior written permission of the publisher, except in the case of brief quotations embodied in critical reviews and certain other noncommercial uses permitted by copyright law.

Limit of Liability/Disclaimer of Warranty: While the publisher and author have used their best efforts in preparing this book, they make no representations or warranties with respect to the accuracy or completeness of the contents of this book and specifically disclaim any implied warranties of merchantability or fitness for a particular purpose. No warranty may be created or extended by sales representatives or written sales materials. The advice and strategies contained herein may not be suitable for your situation. You should consult with a professional where appropriate. Neither the publisher nor author shall be liable for any loss of profit or any other commercial damages, including but not limited to special, incidental, consequential, or other damages

ISBN-13:978-1985808072

ISBN-10:1985808072

DEDICATION

For Cindy,

Pleasant memories, always!

TABLE OF CONTENTS

Other Books By Amy Zackary 10
INTRODUCTION 1
   A Quick Overview Of The Keto Diet 1
   A Quick Overview Of The Vegan Diet 6
   Understanding The Vegan Keto Diet 7
   Tips For Vegan Keto Success 8
   Vegan Ketogenic Macronutrients 9
   Vegan Ketogenic Diet Vegetables 12
RECIPES FOR VEGAN KETOGENIC COOKING 13
BREAKFAST RECIPES 15
   Coconut Cocoa Shake 15
   Coconut Macadamia Cocoa Smoothie 17
   Chia Chocolate Pudding 18
   Flaxseed Waffles 19
   Vegan Pancakes 20
   Vegan Breakfast Bowls 21
   Breakfast Porridge 22
   Overnight Vanilla Oats 23
   Overnight Hemp Pumpkin Oatmeal 24
   Chocolate Avocado Raspberry Smoothie 25
   Breakfast Chia Strawberry Jars 26
   Creamy Spinach Smoothie 27

- Chocolate Pumpkin Cookies 28
- Blueberry Banana-Flavored Bread Smoothie 29
- Tofu Scramble 30

LUNCH RECIPES 31

- Greek Cucumber Salad 32
- Dill Cucumber Salad 33
- Broccoli Soup 34
- Zoodles Salad 35
- Cucumber Avocado Gazpacho 36
- Caesar Salad 37
- Strawberry Spinach Salad 39
- Asian Zucchini Salad 40
- Asian Slaw 41
- Colorful Vegetable Noodles 43
- Avocado Salsa 44

DINNER RECIPES 45

- Cream Of Pumpkin Soup 46
- Vegetable Stew 47
- Red Gazpacho 48
- Cranberry Carrot Salad 50
- Vegetable Soup 51
- Thyme And Cauliflower Soup 53
- Mediterranean Zoodles Pasta 54
- Eggplant Hash 55
- Spinach Tabbouleh 57
- Roasted Zucchini, Eggplant And Mushrooms 59

Roasted Cauliflower 60

Sautéed Mushrooms, Onions And Zucchini 61

Almond Vegetable Mix 62

Avocado Cilantro Salad 64

Blueberry Kale Salad 65

Garden Soup 66

SIDE DISHES 69

Russian Slaw 70

Mint, Apple And Cabbage Slaw 72

Antipasto Artichoke Salad 73

Asparagus, Green Beans And Artichokes Salad 75

Grilled Garlic Lemon Zucchini 76

Pickled Onions 77

Roasted Cauliflower With Cilantro And Lime 78

Jicama And Cucumber Slaw 80

Hemp Cabbage Salad 81

Turnip Fries 82

Vinaigrette Toasted Green Beans 83

Cucumber Salad With Cumin And Lemon 84

Avocado Slaw 85

Cabbage Salad 86

Carrot Chips 87

Cauliflower Rice 88

Sesame Garlic Green Beans 89

SOUPS 91

Broccoli Soup 92

Roasted Tomato Soup 93

Asparagus Soup 95

Pistachio Broccoli Soup 97

Chipotle Pumpkin Soup 98

Basil Zucchini Soup 99

Zoodle Soup 101

Miso Soup 102

Asparagus Hazelnut Soup 104

Creamy Broccoli And Coconut Soup 105

Cremini Mushroom Soup 107

Creamy Green Soup 108

Roasted Garlic Soup 109

Basil Tomato Soup 111

Leek And Onion Soup 113

Yellow Squash Soup 114

APPETIZERS 117

Garlic And Basil Soup 118

Roasted Herbed Olives 119

Zucchini Chips 120

Energy Balls 121

Marinated Mushrooms 122

Vegan Mini Quesadilla 124

Carrot Granola Balls 125

Parsnip Chips 126

Buffalo Cauliflower Wings 127

Cabbage Chips 129

Oat Peanut Butter Energy Balls 130

Roasted Sesame Seeds And Edamame 131

Peanut Butter Balls 132

Pickled Turnips 133

DESSERTS 135

Coconut Chocolate Fat Bombs 136

Matcha Mint Fat Bombs 137

Pumpkin Spice Muffins 138

Dark Chocolate Caramels 140

Blueberry Cobbler 141

Tiger Butter Candies 142

Brownies 144

Chocolate Cake 146

Vegan Truffles 148

Chocolate Chip Pumpkin Cookie 149

Almond Chocolate Smoothie 150

Other Books By Amy Zackary

The Anti-Inflammation Cookbook: Scrumptious Recipes To Fight Inflammatory Diseases & Restore Overall Health

Fatty Liver: Recipes And Guide To Prevent And Reverse Fatty Liver, Lose Weight And Live Longer

INTRODUCTION

A Quick Overview Of The Keto Diet

A keto diet is a low carbohydrate, high fat and moderate protein diet that causes the body to produce ketones in the liver which are then used as energy. When a person consumes high or normal carbohydrate, the body produces glucose and insulin which are easily converted and used by the body as energy. Glucose is the preferred or main energy source that is selected over any other source of energy, while insulin helps to process the glucose in the bloodstream. Here, fats are not needed but are merely stored. However, when the carb intake is lowered, the body enters a state of ketosis. During this state, the body produces ketones, which are the by-products of the broken down fats in the liver. The body initiates ketosis to help people with low food intake survive.

The main objective of a well-structured keto diet is to force the body into this metabolic state. This is accomplished by starving the body of carbohydrates and not calories. Our bodies adjust easily to what it is given. So, once it is devoid of carbohydrate and overloaded with fats, it will start to burn ketosis as its number one energy source for normal day to day functions. Thus, the principle of the ketogenic diet is to restrict carbohydrates to a certain level, in so doing, push the body into the metabolic state known as ketosis, where it will then break the fat molecules down into ketones to use as alternative energy source.

The key features of a ketogenic diet are low amount of dietary carbohydrates and a high amount of dietary fat. The ratio of this diet is 75% dietary fat, 20% proteins and only 5% carbohydrates or around 70% fats, 25% protein, and 5% carbohydrate. However, this ratio can be adjusted for different people. For the body to adjust to this diet and go into ketosis, nutrient intake should be between 25 to 30g of net carbs per day.

What are net carbs? Net carbs are your total dietary carbohydrates, minus dietary fiber and sugar alcohols. Fiber and sugar alcohol do not raise blood sugar because they cannot be broken into glucose. Consequently, most people do not count them towards their total carb count. For example, if 1 cup of broccoli contains 6g of carb and 2 g fiber. The net carb of 1 cup broccoli will be 4g (having subtracted the dietary fiber from the total carb).

Some individuals attain ketosis faster than others. This is also dependent on the individual's body type, levels of activity and what is being eaten. Nevertheless, you can attain ketosis very fast when you exercise on an empty stomach, restrict carbohydrate intake to 20g or less in a day as well as when you consume lots of water. But for a normal person starting a ketogenic diet and eating 25-30g of net carbs daily, the total process of adaptation should take about 2 weeks.

With a ketogenic diet, there will be no need for you to worry about calories as the fats and proteins are filling and will keep you full for an extended period of time. However, if you exercise, you must be more vigilant as exercise comes with a greater calorie deficit that must be replenished.

Be sure to always consult your physician if you have reservations about starting a ketogenic diet. Nevertheless, you MUST see a physician if you come from a family with a history of diabetic or pre-existing conditions because higher intake of protein will definitely put a strain on the kidneys.

Changes In The Body

Your body is accustomed to the straightforward routine of breaking carbohydrates down and using them as energy. To accomplish this process, it has built up a resource of enzymes overtime and has only a handful of enzymes for handling fats. As a result, the body merely stores them.

Now, your body has to handle the increase in fats and the lack of glucose. To do this, it has to build up new enzyme supplies. Once your body is induced to a ketogenic state, it will use up the left over glucose it can find, then switch over to the glycogen in the muscles. This may lead to lack of energy and other minor ailments in the first week such as:

- Headaches
- Dizziness
- Mental fogginess
- Aggravation
- Flu-like symptoms colloquially known as the Keto-Flu

These symptoms are normal and will disappear after a week. It is simply due to your electrolytes being flushed out since the ketosis has a diuretic effect. Ensure you drink lots of water and increase your sodium intake. This will help to replenish the electrolyte and help with water retention as well.

Once the body becomes adapted to keto, it will then be able to fully use the fats as its main source of energy. Athletes on this diet do not need to be afraid of a drop in performance after the first week.

Benefits Of The Keto Diet

Being on a low-carb, high-fat diet comes with numerous benefits. Let's consider a few:

Weight Loss

The ketogenic diet basically uses body fat as an energy source. This is because of the significant drop in the insulin (the hormone responsible for storing fat) levels. Consequently, your body begins to burn its own stored fat for energy, leading to weight loss. Unlike starvation, that often leads to large loss of body protein, mainly from muscle tissue, the keto diet provides quick and easy weight loss, while allowing dieters to eat as much fat as they desire with minimal protein.

This makes weight loss a significant benefit of the ketogenic diet on account of the lower insulin levels and the body's act of burning stored fat. The aim of this diet for weight loss is 'eat fat to lose fat'. Consequently, you will record weight loss every single week of being on the diet, particularly in the first month. You will not be bothered about regaining your lost weight as long as you stick to the keto diet formula of eating high fat, low carb and moderate proteins. Additionally, some blood pressure issues are linked with excess weight, which is a good thing since keto leads to weight loss

Control Blood Sugar

Since the keto diet is selective on the kind of foods to eat, it naturally results in lower blood sugar levels. Studies have shown that this diet compared to low-calorie diets is better at managing and preventing diabetes. Individuals, who are type 2 diabetes but who aren't on insulin, can benefit from the ketogenic diet.

Mental Focus

If you are thinking of increasing your mental performance, consider the ketogenic diet. Ketones, product of this diet, are very good for the brain. Also, lowering carb intake makes it possible to avoid increase in blood sugar which helps you to focus and concentrate significantly.

Normalized Hunger & Increased Energy

Other diets make people feel miserable due to hunger and they eventually give up. But with the low carb, high fat diet, you experience an automatic reduction in appetite; you will eat fewer calories effortlessly and surprisingly feel satisfied. Additionally, you can say good-bye to ups and downs. With the keto diet, you will notice stability in your energy levels. You will always have a full tank of energy to run your day. Your physical performance will be enhanced.

Cholesterol Benefits

Although the ketogenic diet is high in fat, it won't raise your cholesterol or increase your risk for heart disease. This is because the fats are heart-healthy fats or 'good fats' and not trans fats that may lead to inflammation which causes heart disease. The keto diet leads to a significant increase in blood levels of HDL.

Improved Skin Condition

It's common to experience improvements in your skin when you switch to a ketogenic diet. Studies have shown an improvement in acne, skin inflammations and lesions.

A Quick Overview Of The Vegan Diet

A vegan diet is basically the consumption of plant- based foods and the elimination of all animal products. Vegans do not want to harm any living thing. Therefore, unlike vegetarians, they do not eat animal by-products such as eggs and diary. They avoid any foods that are processed with the use of animal products, for instance, refined white sugar. Instead, their diet consists mainly of fruits, vegetables, beans, grains and nuts. Some vegans even go beyond food to adopt a total veganism lifestyle by eliminating clothes, medications and personal care items that use animal products or exploit animals. Veganism was borne out of the need to eliminate animal cruelty, providing them safety and preventing them from any form of harm. Thus we can safely define veganism as an advance form of vegetarian diet that prohibits meat, eggs and dairy products as well as other animal-derived ingredients.

What's acceptable?

- Variety of vegetables
- Fruits
- Herbs, seeds, and nuts,
- Whole grains
- Spices

What's not allowed?

- All Animal proteins, including seafood
- All animal by-products, such as honey, bone broth, cheese, butter and collagen
- Eggs
- Diary
- Animal oils/fats

Understanding The Vegan Keto Diet

keto and vegan are two contradictory eating styles. A vegan diet is typically high carb because carbohydrates form the basis of a vegan diet, which is gotten from fruits, vegetables, wheat and many more. But the keto diet is typically low- carb since the objective is to restrictive carb to the barest minimum and burn fat as its main energy source. Additionally, plants, which constitute the vegan diet, store more starch and sugar, while animals, which a keto dieter includes, store more fat. Nevertheless, to enter into ketosis as a vegan dieter, all glucose must be burned. You will then have to look for plant-based foods that are low in carb and contain enough fat and adequate protein. This isn't so easy because, even commercially, the number of available fatty plants is fewer than starchy or sugary ones.

The vegan ketogenic diet is very restrictive; even more restrictive that the regular vegan or keto diet. However, it is doable. The vegan keto diet aims to prioritize fatty plants foods and exclude those that are too starchy or sugary. With a bit of creativity, this can be done. You will need to get your nutrients from fatty plants and also ensure that you eat the necessary amounts of protein and healthy fats that your body needs to function well. This will include avocados, seeds, nuts and coconut oil. It is also imperative that you reduce the amount of carbs to 35 grams in a day; DO NOT follow the regular keto dieters who aim for about 20 grams; if you do, you won't be able to eat enough nuts and seeds.

The most difficult aspect of the vegan keto diet is the calculation, especially at the beginning. To hit all your macronutrients nutrient goals, you'd have to constantly calculate the amount of protein and carbohydrate that you eat on a daily basis. There are online apps that can help you with that. Additionally, you have to watch your micronutrients and see that you get adequate iron. Since you're on a keto diet, you can get iron from pumpkin seeds, seaweed, spinach, soybeans, tomato paste and most leafy green vegetables. If you do not get enough iron, you will feel tired and sluggish all the time.

Tips For Vegan Keto Success

1. Avoid sugary foods and excessive starchy food.

2. Get enough protein.

3. Ensure you get enough calories without taking in too many carbs since you want to achieve ketosis.

4. To avoid deficiencies of vital minerals, vitamins and iron, get enough supplements for minerals and vitamins.

Vegan Ketogenic Macronutrients

Protein

It is quite challenging getting protein on this diet. This is because the best plants sources of protein usually contain very high starch content, which is unacceptable to you. Thankfully, there are a few acceptable sources such as:

- Tofu, a low carb meat-alternative protein source, however, you still have to get fat from other sources. a low-calorie
- Tempeh
- pumpkin seeds
- chia seeds
- flaxseed
- hazelnut
- plant-based protein powders such as hemp

Avoid: unfermented soy products.

It is very important to monitor protein consumption on a keto diet. Inadequate protein in the body will cause the muscle tissues to break down and bring about other negative effects of amino acid deficiencies. Then again, excessive protein in the body can hamper or impede ketosis because your body will want to convert the extra amino acids into glucose.

As a rule, 1 gram of protein per kilogram of body weight is ideal. Therefore, if for instance, you weigh 160 lb; your daily protein requirement will be 72.5. This calculation is suitable for a fairly inactive person. Someone who is more active will require at least 100 grams of protein per kg

Fats

You'll need healthy fats, such as avocados, coconut, and olives. These are mostly unsaturated fats with smaller amounts of poly- and mono-unsaturated fats. As a vegan keto dieter, your food should contain at least 70% of these healthy fats and very few net carbs. Avocados are the number one choice of low-carb, high-fat dieters. It is a life-saver as it contains 77% fat, 19carbs and 4 percent protein. To get your net carb from this avocado, you'll have to subtract the fiber content from the total carb.

Nuts are another healthy fat source, and this includes macadamias and walnuts. One good thing about these fat sources are the products that can be created out of them, such as coconut flakes and full-fat coconut milk; avocado oil, olive oil and nut butters. These products spur creativity and enables you enjoy variety of meals.

To include fats in a vegan ketogenic diet, eat lots of whole avocado and macadamia nuts as a main fat source, if you can. But if you find it boring, consider using any of the good fat sources as oils for dressing on leafy greens, for instance. Use oils generously for cooking and drizzling over veggies. This makes your meal planning flexible. Since they contain zero carb, you can easily add them to your meals or remove them without disrupting your car count.

These include: Macadamia nuts, Avocado, fruit and oil, Flax seed oil, Coconut oil, Olive oil Coconut butter, Sesame oil, Peanut butter (Organic with no added dairy).

Include oils such as: Coconut Oil, Olive Oil, Flaxseed Oil, Macadamia Oil and avocado oil are oils with monounsaturated and polyunsaturated fats and they are very good for cooking as a result of its high smoke point.

Avoid: Transfat oils which are heavily processed and unnatural fats. This includes: Cottonseed Oil, Sunflower Oil Safflower Oil, Soybean Oil, and Canola Oil.

Carbohydrates

As mentioned earlier, it is advisable to get about 35 grams of carb per day. You should only cut down on this number, if you feel energetic and healthy. And this reduction should be done gradually, as this would enable you find the minimum amount that'll work for you.

Vegan Ketogenic Diet Vegetables

Most vegetables are safe. But ensure you get those with lots of added fat so that you can feel satiated and nourished and will not be tempted to take in carbs.

Vegetables to include are :

- Avocado, Artichokes, Asparagus, Bean Sprouts, Bell peppers, Beet Greens, Bok Choy, Broccoli and Brussel Sprouts.

- Others are Cabbage, Cauliflower, Carrots, Celery root, Dill pickles, Celery, Collard greens, Chives, Cucumber, and Edamame.

- It is also safe to include Mushrooms, Eggplant, Garlic, Fennel, Green Beans, Leeks, Olives, Kale, Onions, Parsley, Lettuce, and Peppers.

- Additionally, Radishes, Spinach, Shallots, Scallions, Spaghetti Squash, Summer squash, Sprouts, Turnips and Zucchini are great!

Avoid these vegetables

- Potatoes
- Corn
- Peas
- Beans
- Parsnips
- Yams
- Yucca

Avoid Fruits:

Avoid all nearly all fruits in the market because of their high carb content. For instance, ripe bananas contain 3% fat, 93% carb and 4% protein. Mango is also a no-no, as it contains more than 90 % carb.

For nuts and seeds

- Almonds
- Chia Seeds
- Hazelnuts
- Pumpkin Seeds
- Sunflower Seeds
- Pecans
- Macadamias
- Coconut Flakes
- Walnuts
- Cashews (a bit higher carb, so do not over-consume)
- Sesame Seeds

Macadamia Nut

RECIPES FOR VEGAN KETOGENIC COOKING

BREAKFAST RECIPES

Coconut Cocoa Shake

Add some pep to your day with this creamy bomb.

Servings: 1-2

Preparation time: 5 minutes

Cooking time: 0 minute

Ingredients:

6-8 ounces of unsweetened coconut milk

4 ounces of full fat coconut milk or cream

1-2 tablespoons of cocoa powder

1-2 tablespoons of melted coconut oil

1/2 tablespoon of sunflower seeds butter

A dash of sea salt

Directions:

1. Blend all the ingredients together in a blender until smooth.

Nutrition Per Serving

Calories: 220, Fat: 16g, Carbohydrates: 5g, Protein: 3g

Coconut Macadamia Cocoa Smoothie

It can also serve as a dessert.

Servings: 1

Preparation time: 5 minutes

Cooking time: 0 minutes

Ingredients:

1 cup of ice cubes

3/4 cup of unsweetened coconut milk

2 tablespoons of sweetener

2 tablespoons of salted macadamia nuts, minced

1 tablespoon of unsweetened cocoa powder

1/2 teaspoon of vanilla extract

A dash of salt

Optional toppings:

Toasted coconut

Macadamia nuts

Directions:

1. Blend all the ingredients in a blender until smooth.

2. Add the toppings if desired and serve.

Nutrition Per Serving

Calories: 412.46, Fat: 44.76g, Carbohydrates: 8.04g, Protein: 5.22g

Chia Chocolate Pudding

Keeps you full for the better part of the day.

Servings: 1

Preparation time: 5 minutes

Cooking time: 0 minutes

Ingredients:

1/2 cup of almond milk or water

1/4 cup of coconut milk

1/4 cup of whole or ground chia seeds

5-10 drops of stevia extract

1 tablespoon of powdered swerve or erythriol

1 tablespoon of unsweetened raw cocoa powder

1/2 tablespoon of raw cocoa nibs

Directions:

1. Combine all the ingredients except the cocoa nibs together. Leave to stand for 10-15 minutes at least or preferably overnight.

2. Top with the cocoa nibs and serve.

Nutrition Per Serving

Calories: 329, Fat: 25.6g, Carbohydrates: 6.3g, Protein: 9.5g

Flaxseed Waffles

It contains no flour and comes out crispy.

Servings: 4

Preparation time: 10 minutes

Cooking time: 25 minutes

Ingredients:

2 cups of golden flaxseed, coarsely ground

1/2 cup of water

1/3 cup of melted coconut oil

5 tablespoons of finely ground flaxseed mixed with 15 tablespoons of warm water

1 tablespoon of baking powder

2 teaspoons of ground cinnamon

1 teaspoon of sea salt

Directions:

1. Preheat the waffle iron over medium heat.

2. In a large bowl, mix the baking powder, flaxseed and salt together. Set aside.

3. Blend the water, finely ground flaxseed mixture and coconut oil in a blender until it foams.

4. Pour this mixture into the baking powder mixture and combine thoroughly with a spatula until it becomes fluffy. Leave to stand for 3 minutes.

5. Stir in the cinnamon and evenly divide the batter into 4 portions.

6. Cook the batter one at a time.

Nutrition Per Serving

Calories: 550, Fat: 42g, Carbohydrates: 3g, Protein: 18.3g

Vegan Pancakes

Add your favorite toppings for a delicious breakfast.

Servings: 1

Preparation time: 10 minutes

Cooking time: 7 minutes

Ingredients:

2 tablespoons of vanilla vegan powder

1 1/2 tablespoons of coconut oil

1 tablespoons of ground flaxseed mixed with 3 tablespoons of water

1 tablespoon of flaxseed, ground

1/4 teaspoon of baking powder

A pinch of salt

Directions:

1. Combine the dry ingredients in a bowl.

2. In another bowl, combine the wet ingredients together.

3. Add the wet ingredients to the dry ingredients and combine thoroughly.

4. Grease a pan lightly and heat over medium heat.

5. Evenly divide the batter into 3 portions and pour into the hot pan.

6. Cook the pancake for 5 minutes on one side, flip and cook for an extra 2 minutes.

Nutrition Per Serving

Calories: 309, Fat: 27.1g, Carbohydrates: 2.2g, Protein: 13.4g

Vegan Breakfast Bowls
Begin your day on the right note with this awesome dish.

Servings: 1

Preparation time: 10 minutes

Cooking time: 0 minutes

Ingredients:

1 medium-sized Hass avocado, halved and pitted

2 tablespoons of tahini

1 small carrot, shredded

Dressing:

1/4 cup of lemon juice

1/4 cup of extra virgin olive oil

1 tablespoon of grated ginger

1 tablespoon of poppy seeds

1/4 teaspoon of salt

Directions:

1. Combine the dressing ingredients in a tightly sealed jar and shake thoroughly.

2. Mix the carrot with 2 tablespoons of the dressing.

3. Scoop the carrot into the avocado and sprinkle the tahini over it.

Nutrition Per Serving

Calories: 562, Fat: 52g, Carbohydrates: 5.5g, Protein: 8g

Breakfast Porridge
Meal prep a batch if this and enjoy stress-free breakfast for a week

Servings: 1

Preparation time: 3 minutes

Cooking time: 5 minutes

Ingredients:

1/2 cup of water

2 tablespoons of almond flour

2 tablespoons of hemp hearts

2 tablespoons of unsweetened coconut, shredded

1 tablespoon of chia seeds

1 tablespoon of flaxseed meal

1/2 teaspoon of pure vanilla extract

1/4 teaspoon of granulated stevia

A pinch of sea salt

Directions:

1. In a small pan, add all the ingredients except the vanilla and stir over low heat.

2. Cook and stir for about 3-5 minutes until it becomes thick.

3. Add the vanilla, stir and serve warm.

Nutrition Per Serving

Calories: 334, Fat: 29g, Carbohydrates: 2g, Protein: 15g

Overnight Vanilla Oats
An easy breakfast that's also lifesaving!

Servings: 2

Preparation time: 15 minutes

Cooking time: 0 minutes

Ingredients:

1/2 cup of hemp hearts

2/3 cup of full fat coconut milk

1 tablespoon of chia seeds

2 teaspoons of erythriol

A pinch of Himalayan rock salt, finely ground

1/2 teaspoon of vanilla extract

Directions:

1. Combine all the ingredients together in a bowl. Cover and refrigerate for at least 8 hours or overnight.

2. Stir in extra milk the next day and serve.

Nutrition Per Serving

Calories: 408, Fat: 34.7g, Carbohydrates: 9.1g, Protein: 15.3g

Overnight Hemp Pumpkin Oatmeal

Start your mornings on the right note with a bowl of oats.

Servings: 1

Preparation time: 2 minutes

Cooking time: 0 minutes

Ingredients:

3 tablespoons of hemp hearts

3 tablespoons of almond milk

1 tablespoon of pumpkin purée

2 drops of liquid stevia

1 teaspoon of chia seeds

1/2 teaspoon of pumpkin pie spice

Directions:

1. Combine all the ingredients thoroughly in a mason jar or bowl.

2. Cover and refrigerate for at least 4 hours or preferably overnight.

Nutrition Per Serving

Calories: 310, Fat: 27g, Carbohydrates: 3g, Protein: 11g

Chocolate Avocado Raspberry Smoothie

Gobble your breakfast on the go.

Servings: 2

Preparation time: 3 minutes

Cooking time: 0 minutes

Ingredients:

1 1/4 cup of cashew milk

1/3 cup of frozen raspberries

1/2 avocado

1 tablespoon of powdered sweetener

1 tablespoon of cocoa powder

1/8 teaspoon of raspberry extract

Directions:

Throw all the ingredients into a blender and process until smooth.

Nutrition Per Serving

Calories: 133, Fat: 9.50g, Carbohydrates: 4.84g, Protein: 2.16

Breakfast Chia Strawberry Jars

Begin your day with a dose of energy.

Servings: 4

Preparation time: 15 minutes

Cooking time: 5 minutes

Ingredients:

1 cup of coconut milk

1 cup of strawberries, sliced

1 cup of coconut milk yogurt

4 tablespoons of whole chia seeds

2 tablespoons of water

1/4 teaspoon of ground ginger

1/4 teaspoon of cinnamon

4 large strawberries, sliced

Liquid stevia, optional

Directions:

1. Cook the 1 cup of strawberry slices with 2 tablespoons of water in a small pan. Simmer and cook for some minutes until it softens. Use either a spatula or fork to break the strawberries, add a few drops of stevia if using and set aside.

2. Combine the ginger, chia seeds, milk, some drops of stevia and cinnamon in a small bowl. Keep aside for 20-30 minutes to soak. Then evenly divide the mixture between 4 jars.

3. Add the cooked strawberries, followed by the sliced strawberries. Ensure that you press it down firmly to the jar sides.

4. Add the coconut milk yogurt as topping.

Nutrition Per Serving

Calories: 230, Fat: 17.9g, Carbohydrates: 7.5g, Protein: 8.7g

Creamy Spinach Smoothie
It is filling and delicious.

Servings: 2

Preparation time: 5 minutes

Cooking time: 0 minutes

Ingredients:

3 1/2 ounces of chopped spinach

1 cup of coconut cream

1/2 cup of frozen berries

1/4 cup of cocoa powder

1 tablespoon of granulated sugar substitute

Directions:

Blend all the ingredients together until smooth.

Nutrition Per Serving

Calories: 362, Fat: 33.5g, Carbohydrates: 7.6g, Protein: 7.5g

Chocolate Pumpkin Cookies

Enjoy with a warm glass of milk.

Servings: 20

Preparation time: 10 minutes

Cooking time: 15 minutes

Ingredients:

1 cup of almond butter

1/2 cup of dark chocolate chips, optional

1/2 cup of pumpkin purée

2 teaspoons of pumpkin pie spice

1/4 teaspoon of sea salt

1/4 cup of maple syrup

1 teaspoon of vanilla extract

Directions:

1. Preheat oven to 350F.

2. Line two baking pans with silpat or parchment paper.

3. In a medium bowl, mix all the ingredients together to form a smooth batter.

4. Fold in the chocolate chips if using.

5. Drop the batter on the prepared baking pan with a spoon and spread out in circles with the back of the spoon.

6. Bake for 12-15 minutes until the cookies' edges are a bit golden.

Nutrition Per Serving

Calories: 95, Fat: 7g, Carbohydrates: 7g, Protein: 3g

Blueberry Banana-Flavored Bread Smoothie

This banana flavored smoothie gives a good hearty satisfying feeling that is just perfect for breakfast.

Servings: 2

Preparation time: minutes

Cooking time:

Ingredients:

3 tablespoons golden flaxseed meal

1 tablespoon chia seeds

10 drop liquid Stevia

2 cups vanilla unsweetened coconut milk

2 tablespoons MCT oil

¼ cup blueberries

1 ½ teaspoons banana extract

¼ teaspoon xanthan gum

Directions:

1. In a blend, add all ingredients.

2. Give it a few minutes to soak and then blend well to incorporate everything.

3. Serve and enjoy!

Nutrition Per Serving

Calories: 270, Fat: 23.31g, Carbohydrates: 4.66g, Protein: 3.13g

Tofu Scramble

Servings: 1

Preparation time: minutes

Cooking time: 2-4 minutes

Ingredients:

1 block firm tofu

½ cup cherry tomatoes or peppers

1 tablespoon of olive oil

½ cup frozen spinach

Onion powder, to taste

Garlic powder, to taste

Salt and pepper, to taste

1 pinch turmeric, for color (optional)

Directions:

1. Add all ingredients to a pan. Sauté on medium or low heat for a couple of minutes

2. Serve and enjoy!

LUNCH RECIPES

Greek Cucumber Salad

A delicious Mediterranean fare.

Servings: 6

Preparation time: 10 minutes

Cooking time: 0 minutes

Ingredients:

1 1/2 ounces of red onion, coarsely chopped

1/2 cup of kalamata olives

1/2 cup of raw cashew

1/2 cup of sun-dried tomatoes

1 avocado, peeled, pit removed and cut into cubes

2 large cucumbers, cut into half lengthwise and sliced

Directions:

Combine all the ingredients in a large bowl and toss with dressing.

Nutrition Per Serving

Calories: 246, Fat: 17.5g, Carbohydrates: 9g, Protein: 9.5g

Dill Cucumber Salad

The combination of flavors in this salad gives it a distinct taste.

Servings: 4

Preparation time: 10 minutes

Cooking time: 0 minutes

Ingredients:

1/4 cup of sprig dill

2 cucumbers, cut into 1/4-inch slices

8 tablespoons of white wine vinegar

2 teaspoons of sweetener

1 teaspoon of salt

Directions:

1. In a medium-sized bowl, mix the dill, vinegar, sweetener and salt together.

2. Add the cucumber and toss gently.

3. Keep in the refrigerator for 30 minutes so that the flavors can come together.

4. Drain any extra liquid and serve.

Nutrition Per Serving

Calories: 24, Fat: 0.2g, Carbohydrates: 5g, Protein: 1g

Broccoli Soup

A creamy soup to fight cold days.

Servings: 4

Preparation time: 10 minutes

Cooking time: 30 minutes

Ingredients:

1 can of full fat coconut milk

3 cups of chopped broccoli florets

3 cups of chopped celery

2 cups of vegetable broth

1/2 teaspoon of garlic pepper

1/2 teaspoon of onion powder

Red pepper flakes

Salt

Pepper

Directions:

1. Add the milk, broccoli, celery, broth, garlic pepper, onion powder and red pepper flakes to a pot. Cook for about 30 minutes over medium heat until the broccoli and celery softens.

2. Pour the soup into a blender and process until smooth.

Nutrition Per Serving

Calories: 200, Fat: 17g, Carbohydrates: 5g, Protein: 4g

Zoodles Salad

A vegan delight made with walnuts and parmesan.

Servings: 4

Preparation time: 15 minutes

Cooking time: 0 minutes

Ingredients:

Dressing:

1/3 cup of avocado oil

1/4 cup of lemon juice, freshly squeezed

1 teaspoon of fresh garlic, crushed

1/2 teaspoon of granulated sugar substitute

Pepper

Kosher salt

Salad:

4 cups of zucchini, spiralized

1 cup of fresh radicchio, shredded

1 ounce of shaved vegan Parmesan cheese

1/4 cup of coarsely chopped walnuts

1/4 cup of coarsely chopped parsley

Directions:

1. Whisk the dressing ingredients in a small bowl.

2. In a medium bowl, gently mix the salad ingredients together.

3. Drizzle the dressing over the salad and toss to coat.

Nutrition Per Serving

Calories: 265, Fat: 25g, Carbohydrates: 5.5g, Protein: 6g

Cucumber Avocado Gazpacho

Cool down on hot summer afternoons with this cold soup.

Servings: 6

Preparation time: 15 minutes

Cooking time: 0 minutes

Ingredients:

1 1/2 cups of water

1/3 cup of loosely packed basil or cilantro leaves

1/4 cup of apple cider vinegar

2 medium-sized cucumbers, peeled, seeded and chopped

2 garlic cloves, chopped

1 jalapeño, seed removed and chopped

1 1/2 avocados, chopped

1 teaspoon of salt

3/4 teaspoon of pepper

Directions:

1. Process the avocado, cucumbers, basil, jalapeño, garlic, vinegar, salt and pepper in a food processor or blender until smooth.

2. Pour in water and blend together.

3. Season with salt and pepper.

Nutrition Per Serving

Calories: 95, Fat: 6.3g, Carbohydrates: 8.34g, Protein: 1.67g

Caesar Salad

Ready at the snap of a finger.

Servings: 4

Preparation time: 5 minutes

Cooking time: 0 minutes

Ingredients:

12 cups of romaine leaves, chopped

1/4 cup of hemp seeds

1 ripe avocado

3 garlic cloves, crushed

3 tablespoons of lemon juice

2 tablespoons of water

1 tablespoon of capers

1 tablespoon of caper brine

2 teaspoons of Dijon mustard

Sea salt

Freshly ground pepper

Directions:

1. Blend all the ingredients except the hemp seeds and romaine in a blender or food processor until smooth.

2. Pour into a bowl, add the hemp seeds and stir.

3. In a large bowl, place the romaine leaves, add the blended mixture and combine with the leaves to coat.

Nutrition Per Serving

Calories: 168, Fat: 12.5g, Carbohydrates: 5.2g, Protein: 6.6g

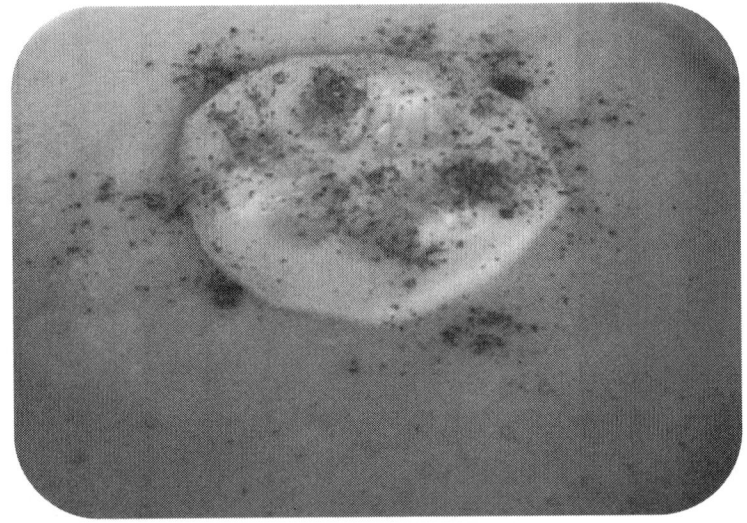

Cucumber Avocado Gazpacho

Strawberry Spinach Salad

It's flavorful, colorful and yummy.

Servings: 4

Preparation time: 10 minutes

Cooking time: 0 minutes

Ingredients:

For the salad:

5 ounces of baby spinach

1/4 cup of sliced almonds

1 cup of sliced strawberries

For the dressing:

1/4 cup of olive or avocado oil

2 tablespoons of red wine vinegar

1/2 teaspoon of vanilla stevia

1/8 teaspoon of garlic powder

1/8 teaspoon of paprika

1/8 teaspoon of salt

Directions:

1. Combine all the salad ingredients in a medium bowl.

2. Whisk the dressing ingredients together and drizzle over the salad.

Nutrition Per Serving

Calories: 75, Fat: 5g, Carbohydrates: 6.3g, Protein: 2.7g

Asian Zucchini Salad

A nice, crunchy and filling salad

Servings: 10

Preparation time: 10 minutes

Cooking time: 0 minutes

Ingredients:

1 pound of cabbage, shredded

1 cup of almonds, sliced

1 cup of shelled sunflower seeds

1/3 cup of rice, white or cider vinegar

3/4 cup of avocado oil

1 medium-sized zucchini, spiralized thinly

1 teaspoon of stevia drops

Directions:

1. Use a knife or kitchen shears to chop the zucchini into smaller pieces. Keep aside.

2. Mix the sunflower seeds, cabbage and almonds together in a large bowl.

3. Add the zucchini and stir to combine.

4. Use a fork to whisk the vinegar, stevia and oil in a small bowl.

5. Drizzle the dressing over the salad and toss to coat.

6. Refrigerate for 2 hours at the before serving.

Nutrition Per Serving

Calories: 120, Fat: 9.3g, Carbohydrates: 7.3g, Protein: 4g

Asian Slaw

An attractive and enticing lunch idea.

Servings: 6

Preparation time: 15 minutes

Cooking time: 0 minutes

Ingredients:

1 cup of snow peas, sliced into thin sticks

1/4 cup of rice wine vinegar

4 whole scallions

4 cloves of garlic, crushed

2 small red bell peppers, seeded and thinly sliced

1 small head of Napa cabbage, shredded

1 large carrot, peeled and sliced into thin sticks

1 medium red onion, thinly sliced

2 tablespoons of sweetener

2 tablespoons of sesame oil

2 tablespoons of black sesame seeds

1 tablespoon of chopped fresh ginger

Salt

Pepper

Directions:

1. Combine all the ingredients in a large bowl.

2. Allow to stand for about 10 minutes.

3. Toss again and serve.

Nutrition Per Serving

Calories: 132.41, Fat: 6.59g, Carbohydrates: 7.9g, Protein: 2.95g

Spiralized Zucchini

Colorful Vegetable Noodles

It is beautiful, fun and perfect for lunch.

Servings: 6

Preparation time: 15 minutes

Cooking time: 20 minutes

Ingredients:

6 ounces of mixed bell peppers, thinly sliced

4 ounces of red onion, thinly sliced

3 large garlic cloves, thinly sliced

4 tablespoons of oil

1 medium summer squash, spiralized

1 medium zucchini, spiralized

1 large carrot, spiralized

Salt

Pepper

Directions:

1. Preheat oven to 400°F.

2. Coat a baking pan with oil.

3. Mix the vegetables together in a bowl and season with a sprinkle of salt and pepper.

4. Transfer the vegetables to the baking pan and spread it out in a thin layer.

5. Bake for 20 minutes. Toss halfway while cooking.

Nutrition Per Serving

Calories: 48, Fat: 0.5g, Carbohydrates: 7g, Protein: 1.5g

Avocado Salsa

Keep hunger at bay with this nourishing recipe.

Servings: 8

Preparation time: 10 minutes

Cooking time: 0 minutes

Ingredients:

4 avocados, peeled and chopped

2 tomatoes, finely chopped

1 fresh chili, finely chopped

1 lemon, juiced

1 red onion, finely chopped

Directions:

Combine all the ingredients in a bowl.

Nutrition Per Serving

Calories: 178, Fat: 14g, Carbohydrates: 5g, Protein: 2g

DINNER RECIPES

Cream Of Pumpkin Soup

An extremely creamy and velvety soup made with just 4 ingredients.

Servings: 4

Preparation time: 5 minutes

Cooking time: 45 minutes

Ingredients:

2 cups of roasted pumpkin

2 cups of vegetable stock

1/2 cup of cashew cream

1 teaspoon of onion powder

Directions:

1. Add the vegetable stock, onion powder and pumpkin to a large pan. Mix and cook over high heat.

2. Bring to a boil and reduce heat to medium low.

3. Cover the pan and leave to simmer for 30 minutes.

4. Meanwhile, whip the cream until it forms soft peaks, cover and keep in the refrigerator.

5. Blend the soup until smooth after the 30 minutes has elapsed.

6. Pout in the chilled cream and gently whisk to combine.

Nutrition Per Serving

Calories: 209, Fat: 16.7g, Carbohydrates: 9.2g, Protein: 5.3g

Vegetable Stew

A hearty and elegant bowl.

Servings: 8

Preparation time: 15 minutes

Cooking time: 2 hours

Ingredients:

1 15-oz can of fire-roasted diced tomatoes

4 cups of water

3 cups of kale, chopped

2 cups of vegetable broth

2 cups of celery, chopped

1/2 cup of mushroom stems and pieces

1 medium onion, chopped

2 tablespoons of virgin coconut oil

1 tablespoon of black pepper

1 teaspoon of sage

1 teaspoon of dried rosemary

1 teaspoon of oregano leaf

1/2 teaspoon of garlic, minced

1/4 teaspoon of salt

Directions:

1. Add all the ingredients to a stick pot, stir, uncover and bring to a fast boil over high heat. Cook for 10 minutes.

2. Turn down heat to medium and cook for an 15 minutes.

3. Uncover and cook for an extra 15 minutes.

4. Gently stir and reduce heat to low. Cover and simmer for 1 1/2 hours in order for the flavors to blend.

5. Remove from heat and serve.

Nutrition Per Serving

Calories: 73, Fat: 3.7g, Carbohydrates: 6.6g, Protein: 1.9g

Red Gazpacho
Enjoy this light Spanish delicacy for dinner.

Servings: 6

Preparation time: 20 minutes

Cooking time: 20 minutes

Ingredients:

1 cup of extra virgin olive oil

2-4 tablespoons of chopped fresh parsley

2-4 tablespoons of chopped fresh basil

2 tablespoons of wine or apple cider vinegar

2 tablespoons of fresh lemon juice

4-5 medium tomatoes, quartered

2 medium spring onions, sliced

2 garlic cloves, peeled

2 medium avocados, peeled, halved and seeded

1 large cucumber, diced

1 large red pepper, halved, cored and seeded

1 large green pepper, halved, cored and seeded

1 small red onion, peeled and roughly chopped

1 teaspoon of salt

Freshly ground black pepper

Directions:

1. Preheat oven to 400F and line a baking pan with parchment paper.

2. Place the green and red peppers on the baking pan with its cut side facing down and roast in the oven for about 20 minutes or until it begins to blacken and its skin blisters. Remove and keep aside to cool. Peel the skin and discard.

3. Process the red onion, tomatoes, avocados, roasted peppers, parsley, basil, lemon juice, olive oil, garlic, vinegar, salt and pepper in a blender until smooth.

4. Add the spring onions and cucumber; mix with the soup to combine.

5. Adjust seasoning if desired.

Nutrition Per Serving

Calories: 528, Fat: 50.8g, Carbohydrates: 8.5g, Protein: 7.5g

Cranberry Carrot Salad

Cranberry Carrot Salad

Make meal times fun with this colorful salad.

Servings: 4

Preparation time: 15 minutes

Cooking time: 0 minutes

Ingredients:

6 ounces of Napa cabbage, finely shredded

6 ounces of carrot, roughly grated

1/2 cup of frozen cranberries, thawed

10 drops of liquid stevia

1/2 teaspoon of unrefined sea salt

Directions:

1. Lightly mince the cranberries in a small bowl with a fork.

2. Add the stevia and salt; combine thoroughly.

3. Lightly mix the cabbage and carrot in a large bowl.

4. Add the mixed cranberries and combine together.

5. Put in an airtight container and keep in the refrigerator for some hours to allow the flavors blend.

Nutrition Per Serving

Calories: 23, Fat: 0.3g, Carbohydrates: 3.9g, Protein: 1.1g

Vegetable Soup
Packed with vitamins and minerals.

Servings: 8

Preparation time: 10 minutes

Cooking time: 40 minutes

Ingredients:

4 cups of water

2 cups of celery, sliced

2 cups of low sodium vegetable stock

2 cups of fresh spinach, chopped

1 cup of carrot, sliced

1 cup of onion, chopped

1 cup of frozen green beans

2 teaspoons of olive oil

2 large garlic cloves, crushed

1/2 teaspoon of salt

1/2 teaspoon of garlic powder

1/4 teaspoon of pepper

Directions:

1. Heat oil in a Dutch oven over medium heat and sauté the garlic until fragrant.

2. Sauté the celery, carrot and onion for about 10 minutes until the vegetables are soft.

3. Add the water and stock; allow to come to a boil.

4. Add the green beans, garlic powder, salt and pepper.

5. Cover, turn down the heat and simmer for 30 minutes.

6. Remove cover, add the parsley and spinach.

7. Cook for about 5 minutes until the spinach wilts.

Nutrition Per Serving

Calories: 44, Fat: 2g, Carbohydrates: 6g, Protein: 2g

Thyme And Cauliflower Soup
It is warm, comforting and satisfying.

Servings: 6

Preparation time: 10 minutes

Cooking time: 20 minutes

Ingredients:

1 head of cauliflower, chopped into florets

3 cups of vegetable broth

5 cloves of garlic, chopped

1 tablespoon of olive oil

2 teaspoon of thyme powder

1 teaspoon of ground black pepper

1 teaspoon of Celtic sea salt

1/2 teaspoon of match green tea powder

Directions:

1. Heat the broth, match a powder and thyme in a large pot over medium high heat; allow to come to a boil.

2. Add the cauliflower and cook for about 10 minutes until it is soft.

3. Meanwhile, heat oil in a small pan and sauté the garlic for about 1 minute until fragrant.

4. Add the sautéed garlic, salt and pepper to the pot when the cauliflower becomes soft. Cook for an additional 1-2 minutes.

6. Remove from heat, transfer to an immersion blender and blend until smooth.

Nutrition Per Serving

Calories: 51, Fat: 2.4g, Carbohydrates: 6.7g, Protein: 1.5g

Mediterranean Zoodles Pasta
It's fast and easy to prepare.

Servings: 4

Preparation time: 10 minutes

Cooking time: 13 minutes

Ingredients:

1 cup of packed spinach

1/4 cup of sun-dried tomatoes

2 tablespoons of Italian flat leaf parsley, chopped

2 tablespoons of vegan butter

2 tablespoons of capers

2 tablespoons of olive oil

10 kalamata olives, halved

5 garlic cloves, minced

2 large zucchinis, spiralized

Sea salt

Black pepper

Directions:

1. Cook the spinach, zucchini, salt, oil, pepper, garlic and butter in a large pot over medium heat until the spinach wilts and the zucchini softens. Drain the excess liquid.

2. Add the capers, tomatoes, olives and parsley. Stir and cook for 2-3 minutes.

Nutrition Per Serving

Calories: 231, Fat: 20g, Carbohydrates: 6.5g, Protein: 6.5g

Eggplant Hash
A North African inspired dish.

Servings: 8

Preparation time: 15 minutes

Cooking time: 15 minutes

Ingredients:

1/2 cup of sun-dried tomatoes in oil, drained and chopped

1/4 cup of toasted silvered almonds

1/4 cup of whole fresh mint leaves

2 tablespoons of light oil

4 garlic cloves, crushed

2 small red bell peppers, seeded and cut into cubes

1 large eggplant globe, peeled, cut into cubes and salted

1 medium red onion, chopped

1/2 teaspoon of ground coriander seed

14 teaspoon of powdered cayenne pepper

Salt

Freshly cracked pepper

Directions:

1. Preheat a large wok or sauté pan over high heat.

2. Add the oil, lift the pan and swirl it to coat with the oil.

3. Sauté the bell peppers and eggplant for about 1 minute. Toss and spread the veggies in the pan for an additional 1 minute so they can sear.

4. Add the garlic and onion; cook for about 2 minutes.

5. Add salt and pepper; toss and spread the vegetables for 1-2 minutes so that they can sear.

6. Add the mint leaves, tomatoes and almonds; toss to combine.

7. Adjust seasoning and add the spices.

8. Give one last stir and serve.

Nutrition Per Serving

Calories: 99.86, Fat: 6.4g, Carbohydrates: 8.9g, Protein: 2.42g

Spinach Tabbouleh

The cauliflower rice acts as a substitute for the traditional grains.

Servings: 3-4

Preparation time: 15 minutes

Cooking time: 5 minutes

Ingredients:

3 cups of cauliflower rice

3 cups of spinach, chopped

1 cup of regular or cherry tomatoes, chopped

1 cup of fresh parsley, chopped

1/2 cup of fresh lemon juice

1/2 cup of fresh mint, chopped

1/2 cup of extra virgin olive oil

2 tablespoons or extra virgin coconut oil

2 medium spring onions, chopped

1 medium cucumber, peeled and chopped

1 garlic clove, crushed

1 teaspoon of salt

1/4 teaspoon of freshly ground black pepper

Directions:

1. Heat oil in a pan over medium heat.

2. Cook the cauliflower and a pinch of salt for about 5 minutes or until it is tender and crispy while stirring occasionally. Remove from heat, keep aside to cool.

3. Add the vegetables and cooked cauliflower to a salad bowl. Mix well.

4. Whisk the garlic, lemon juice and olive oil in a bowl. Pour this mixture over the tabbouleh.

5. Add seasoning and toss with tongs or two forks to combine.

Nutrition Per Serving

Calories: 245, Fat: 23.5g, Carbohydrates: 5.4g, Protein: 2.6g

Roasted Zucchini, Eggplant And Mushrooms

A savory and yummy dish.

Servings: 6

Preparation time: 15 minutes

Cooking time: 40 minutes

Ingredients:

8 ounces of cremini mushrooms, cut into quarters

1/4 cup of olive oil

2 tablespoons of dried onion flakes

2 tablespoons of balsamic vinegar

6 garlic cloves, crushed

3 fresh rosemary sprigs, chopped

2 medium zucchini, cut into halves lengthwise and sliced

1 medium eggplant, cut into cubes

2 teaspoons of sea salt

1 teaspoon of black pepper

Directions:

1. Preheat oven to 400F.

2. Get a rimmed baking pan and line it with parchment paper or aluminum foil.

3. Mix all the ingredients in a bowl and toss to thoroughly coat the vegetables.

4. Transfer the mixture to the prepared baking pan and evenly spread it in a single layer.

5. Roast the mixture for 40 minutes. Toss every 10 minutes.

Nutrition Per Serving

Calories: 101, Fat: 9g, Carbohydrates: 4.6g, Protein: 1.3g

Roasted Cauliflower
Another great use for the cauliflower.

Servings: 6

Preparation time: 10 minutes

Cooking time: 45 minutes

Ingredients:

1 head of cauliflower

1 garlic clove, minced

1 stick of vegan butter, melted

1 tablespoon of dried parsley

1 tablespoon of lemon zest

1/4 teaspoon of mustard powder

Directions:

1. Remove the stem bottom and leaves from the cauliflower; cut a deep cross into its stem to enable it cook evenly. Place in a baking pan.

2. In a bowl, mix the herbs, mustard, butter and garlic together.

3. Brush the herb mixture over the cauliflower.

4. Roast for 350F while brushing with the herb mixture occasionally.

Nutrition Per Serving

Calories: 150, Fat: 13.6g, Carbohydrates: 5.1g, Protein: 2.2g

Sautéed Mushrooms, Onions And Zucchini

Will leave you craving for more.

Servings: 3

Preparation time: 10 minutes

Cooking time: 10 minutes

Ingredients:

1 cup of fresh mushrooms, thinly sliced

3 tablespoons of low sodium vegetable broth

1 tablespoon of olive oil

1 1/2 tsp of fresh dill, chopped

3 small zucchinis, thinly sliced

1/2 medium onion, thinly sliced

A dash of salt

Pepper

Directions:

1. Heat oil in a medium skillet and sauté the onion until translucent.

2. Add the mushrooms and cook until it starts to get dry.

3. Add the zucchini and broth to the skillet; cook and stir occasionally until the zucchini and mushrooms are cooked.

4. Sprinkle with dill and serve.

Nutrition Per Serving

Calories: 80.4, Fat: 5.0g, Carbohydrates: 7.1g, Protein: 3.7g

Almond Vegetable Mix

Made for busy weeknights.

Servings: 2

Preparation time: 10 minutes

Cooking time: 2 minutes

Ingredients:

For the dressing:

2 tablespoons of extra virgin olive oil

1 tablespoon of organic lemon juice

6 basil leaves, minced

1 garlic clove, minced

1 teaspoon of white vinegar

1/2 teaspoon of black pepper

1/2 teaspoon of Himalayan salt

For the salad:

1 cup of baby spinach

1 cup of spring mix leaves

5 cherry tomatoes

4 asparagus, stem discarded, cut in half

2 radish leaves, sliced

1/4 yellow bell pepper, sliced

1/4 cucumber, sliced

2 tablespoons of almond ricotta cheese

Directions:

1. Combine all the dressing ingredients in a small bowl. Set aside.

2. Boil water in a small pot and cook the asparagus for 4 minutes. Drain.

3. Combine the spring mix and spinach in a large bowl, add the radish, cucumber, bell pepper, asparagus sticks, and cherry tomatoes. Top with the almond cheese.

4. Drizzle the dressing over the salad.

Nutrition Per Serving

Calories: 208, Fat: 18.38g, Carbohydrates: 9.26g, Protein: 4.4g

Avocado Cilantro Salad

A delicious combo that has healthy fats.

Servings: 3

Preparation time: 10 minutes

Cooking time: 0 minutes

Ingredients:

For the dressing:

3 cilantro stems, chopped

2 tablespoons of extra light olive oil

1 tablespoon of lemon juice

1/2 teaspoon of black pepper

1/2 teaspoon of Himalayan salt

1/4 teaspoon of garlic powder

For the salad:

8 cherry tomatoes, diced

1 avocado, cut into cubes

1/2 yellow pepper, diced

1/2 red onion, diced

1/2 cucumber, diced

Directions:

1. Mix all the dressing ingredients in a small bowl.

2. In a large bowl, combine all the salad ingredients and toss with the dressing.

Nutrition Per Serving

Calories: 212, Fat: 19.01g, Carbohydrates: 4.7g, Protein: 2.25g

Blueberry Kale Salad
It is light and amazing.

Servings: 2

Preparation time: 5 minutes

Cooking time: 0 minutes

Ingredients:

10 blueberries

6 ounces of kale, coarsely chopped

1/4 red onion, thinly sliced

2 tablespoons of olive oil

1 tablespoon of almonds, sliced

1 tablespoon of lemon juice

1 tablespoon of parsley

Salt

Pepper

Directions:

Combine all the ingredients in a bowl.

Nutrition Per Serving

Calories: 191, Fat: 16g, Carbohydrates: 9g, Protein: 4g

Garden Soup
You can either serve it hot or cold.

Servings: 8

Preparation time: 10 minutes

Cooking time: 20 minutes

Ingredients:

3 1/2 cups of vegetable stock

3 cups of fresh tomatoes, chopped

1 cup of fresh or frozen peas

1 cup of onion, chopped

1 cup of fresh or frozen green beans, cut

1 cup of zucchini, sliced

2 tablespoons of olive oil

4-6 cloves of garlic, crushed

1 teaspoon of dried basil

1/2 teaspoon of fresh dill, minced

1/4 teaspoon of dried tarragon

1/4 teaspoon of salt, optional

1/4 teaspoon of pepper

Directions:

1. Heat oil in a large saucepan and sauté the onion until soft.

2. Add the garlic and sauté for an additional minute.

3. Add the beans, tomatoes, tarragon, dill, basil, pepper and salt if using. Stir and leave to boil.

4. Lower heat, uncover and simmer for 10 minutes.

5. Pour in the stock, zucchini and peas. Simmer the soup for 5-10 minutes or until the veggies are tender and crispy.

Nutrition Per Serving

Calories: 86, Fat: 5g, Carbohydrates: 10g, Protein: 4g

Kale Blueberry Salad

SIDE DISHES

Russian Slaw

Goes with almost any dish.

Servings: 6

Preparation time: 15 minutes

Cooking time: 0 minutes

Ingredients:

For the salad:

1/2 fennel bulb, halved and thinly sliced

1/2 celeriac, peeled and grated

1/4 small head of red cabbage, halved and thinly sliced

1/4 medium head of white or green cabbage, halved and thinly sliced

For the dressing:

1/3 cup of vegan mayonnaise

2 tablespoons of chives, freshly chopped

2 tablespoons of coconut milk

2 tablespoons of lemon juice, freshly squeezed

1 tablespoon of sriracha chili sauce

1 medium pickled cucumber, finely grated

1 teaspoon of horseradish, freshly grated

1/4 teaspoon of salt

Freshly ground black pepper

Directions:

1. To make the dressing: combine all the dressing ingredients thoroughly in a bowl.

2. Add the salad ingredients to a large bowl, drizzle the dressing over it and mix together.

Nutrition Per Serving

Calories: 131, Fat: 11.1, Carbohydrates: 5.6g, Protein: 1.7g

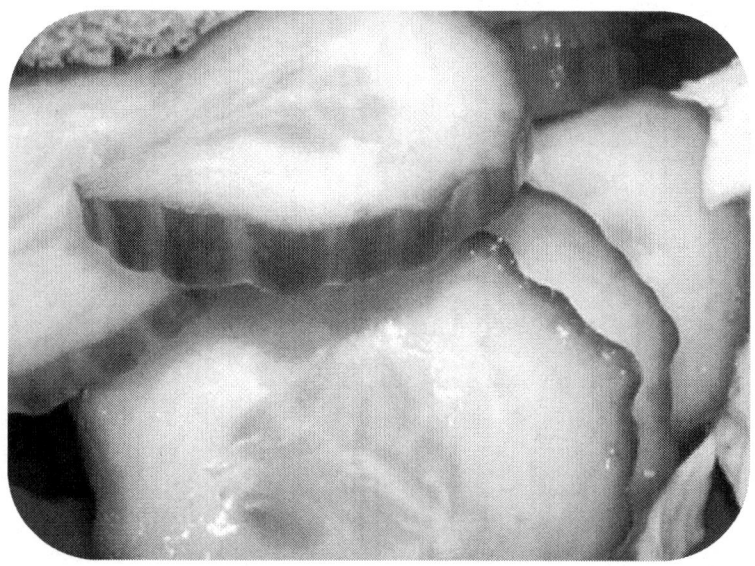

Cucumber Salad

Mint, Apple And Cabbage Slaw
Its taste is absolutely divine.

Servings: 10

Preparation time: 15 minutes

Cooking time: 0 minutes

Ingredients:

8 cups of red cabbage, shredded

2 cups of Granny Smith apples, raw &chopped

1/4 cup of avocado oil

1/4 cup of chopped fresh mint

2 tablespoons of apple cider vinegar

1 tablespoon of lemon juice

1 tablespoon of sugar substitute, granulated

Directions:

1. Toss the chopped apples with the lemon juice to ensure that they do not turn brown.

2. Add to a large salad bowl and mix with the mint and cabbage.

3. In a small bowl, whisk the vinegar, sweetener and oil together.

4. Drizzle the dressing over the salad and toss to coat.

Nutrition Per Serving

Calories: 80, Fat: 6g, Carbohydrates: 5.5g, Protein: 1g

Antipasto Artichoke Salad

It is super healthy and easy to make.

Servings: 4

Preparation time: 15 minutes

Cooking time: 35 minutes

Ingredients:

6 cups of water

1/4 cup of green olives, pitted and sliced

1/4 cup of extra virgin olive oil

1/4 cup of jarred cherry peppers, halved

6 baby artichokes

1 tablespoon of chopped fresh dill

1 tablespoon of lemon juice

1 tablespoon of capers, drained

1 tablespoon of fresh lemon juice

2 teaspoons of no-sugar balsamic vinegar

1 1/2 tsp kosher salt, divided

1/4 teaspoon of fresh lemon zest

1/4 teaspoon of caper brine

1/4 teaspoon of granulated sugar substitute, optional

1/4 teaspoon of ground black pepper

Directions:

1. In a medium pot, mix the water with fresh lemon juice and 1 teaspoon of salt.

2. Trim the artichokes off its tough outer leaves and cut in half. Scoop out its hairy center while remaining its smooth white heart.

3. Trim the stems if the artichokes to about a length of 1-inch and then cut off any stringy parts from the stem.

4. Add the prepared artichokes to the pot and bring to a boil.

5. Allow to simmer for 20-30 minutes or until the artichokes are soft enough to be pierced with a fork. Drain.

6. In a medium bowl, combine the remaining ingredients vigorously.

7. Gently toss the artichokes with the mixture to combine.

8. Leave to sit for 10 minutes at least before serving.

Nutrition Per Serving

Calories: 170, Fat: 13g, Carbohydrates: 5g, Protein: 1g

Asparagus, Green Beans And Artichokes Salad
Simply irresistible.

Servings: 4

Preparation time: 15 minutes

Cooking time: 5 minutes

Ingredients:

8 whole artichoke hearts in oil, drained and each cut into 8 wedges

1/2 pound of green beans, ends trimmed, cut into thin strips

1 bunch of asparagus, fibrous ends removed, cut into thin strips

1/4 cup of toasted pine nuts

1/4 cup of extra virgin olive oil, divided

2 cloves of garlic, minced

2 tablespoons of fresh lemon juice

1 tablespoon of capers, drained and roughly chopped

2 teaspoons of fresh rosemary, thyme or oregano, coarsely chopped

Salt

Pepper

Directions:

1. Boil a gallon of water in a medium pot and add about a 1/4 cup of salt.

2. Meanwhile fill a medium bowl halfway with ice water and set a food strainer or colander in a sink.

3. Add the asparagus and green beans to the boiling water. Submerge and cook for about 30-45 seconds.

4. Pour the contents through the colander immediately and then put the drained vegetables in the ice water to cool completely.

5. Mix the remaining ingredients in a medium bowl.

6. Drain the excess water from the asparagus and green beans; add them to the bowl.

7. Season with salt and pepper; toss to combine.

Nutrition Per Serving

Calories: 276.09, Fat: 28.06g, Carbohydrates: 7.94g, Protein: 4.96g

Grilled Garlic Lemon Zucchini
Basic ingredients with awesome flavors.

Servings: 4

Preparation time: 10 minutes

Cooking time: 10 minutes

Ingredients:

1/4 cup of melted vegan butter

3 garlic cloves, crushed

2 medium zucchinis, diagonally cut into 1/2-inch slices

1 lemon, juiced

2 tablespoons of fresh parsley leaves, chopped

1 teaspoon of Italian seasoning

Kosher salt

Freshly ground black pepper

Directions:

1. Whisk all the ingredients, except the zucchini slices, in a small bowl.

2. Brush the whisked mixture on the zucchini.

3. Preheat a grill pan over medium high heat.

4. Place the zucchini slices in a single layer and cook for about 2 minutes on each side until it starts to soften and its sides are seared.

5. Garnish with parsley and serve.

Nutrition Per Serving

Calories: 125.3, Fat: 11.8g, Carbohydrates: 5.2g, Protein: 1.5g

Pickled Onions
It goes well with absolutely anything.

Servings: 8

Preparation time: 10 minutes

Cooking time: 0 minutes

Ingredients:

1 medium red onion, thinly sliced

1/4 cup of fresh lime juice

1 jalapeño chilies, seeded and thinly sliced

1 teaspoon of salt

Directions:

1. Mix all the ingredients in a small bowl.

2. Cover and keep refrigerated for 30 minutes at least or overnight.

Nutrition Per Serving

Calories: 7.66, Fat: 0.01g, Carbohydrates: 1.96g, Protein: 0.17g

Roasted Cauliflower With Cilantro And Lime
The taste is divine!

Servings: 4

Preparation time: 10 minutes

Cooking time: 30 minutes

Ingredients:

1 head of cauliflower, leaves removed and bottom trimmed

2 tablespoons of ground coriander

1/2 lime

1/2 red finger chili, sliced

1 tablespoon of coconut oil, warm

Sprigs of cilantro

Sea salt

Freshly ground black pepper

Directions:

1. Preheat oven to 400F.

2. Chop the cauliflower into large florets and place on a rimmed baking pan in a single layer.

3. Drizzle the oil over the florets, allow the oil to flow down the sides.

4. Dust the florets with coriander and sprinkle the sea salt over it.

5. Roast in the oven for about 30 minutes until both the top and bottom of the cauliflower is brown.

6. Add the red chilis topping and squeeze the lime juice over it.

7. Add the cilantro on top, season with salt and pepper.

Nutrition Per Serving

Calories: 80, Fat: 4g, Carbohydrates: 9g, Protein: 3g

Jicama And Cucumber Slaw

Enjoy with your choice dip or even on its own.

Servings: 8

Preparation time: 10 minutes

Cooking time: 0 minutes

Ingredients:

1/2 English cucumber, cut into matchsticks

1/2 medium-sized jicama, peeled and cut into matchsticks

Dressing:

2 tablespoons of rice vinegar plus 1 teaspoon

2 teaspoons of canola oil

2 teaspoons of sesame oil

1 teaspoon of fresh lime juice

1/4 teaspoon of red pepper flakes

3/4 teaspoon of agave nectar

1/8 teaspoon of salt

Directions:

1. Whisk all the dressing ingredients in a small bowl.

2. Mix the cucumber and jicama in a medium bowl and toss with the dressing.

Nutrition Per Serving

Calories: 83, Fat: 5g, Carbohydrates: 10g, Protein: 1g

Hemp Cabbage Salad

Pretty and awesomely healthy.

Servings: 2-3

Preparation time: 10 minutes

Cooking time: 0 minutes

Ingredients:

3 cups of mixed purple and green cabbage, finely shredded

1/4 cup of hemp seeds

1/4 cup of yellow and red peppers chopped

3 tablespoons of hemp oil

3 tablespoons of chopped cilantro

1 1/2 tablespoons of lime juice

1 1/2 avocados, pitted and chopped

Directions:

Mix all the ingredients together in a large bowl.

Nutrition Per Serving

Calories: 381, Fat: 36g, Carbohydrates: 8.7g, Protein: 6.6g

Turnip Fries

Its crunchiness makes this a favorite.

Servings: 4

Preparation time: 5 minutes

Cooking time: 25 minutes

Ingredients:

2 turnips, peeled and cut into fries

Pepper

1 tablespoon of olive oil

Salt

Directions:

1. Preheat oven to 400F.

2. Grease a baking pan with cooking spray or line it with parchment paper.

3. Combine the ingredients in a bowl and toss to coat.

4. Place the fries in the baking pan in a single layer.

5. Bake for 25 minutes until crispy and done. Flip once after 15 minutes.

Nutrition Per Serving

Calories: 55, Fat: 4g, Carbohydrates: 6g, Protein: 1g

Vinaigrette Toasted Green Beans

Simple to prepare.

Servings: 6

Preparation time: 10 minutes

Cooking time: 10 minutes

Ingredients:

1 pound of fresh green beans

1/3 cup of chopped walnuts

1/4 cup of olive oil

2 teaspoons of Dijon mustard

2-3 garlic cloves

Salt

Pepper

Directions:

1. Steam the beans.

2. Meanwhile heat oil in a pan and sauté the garlic for 1 minute.

3. Add the mustard and chopped walnuts to the pan. Cook for an extra 2 minutes until the walnuts are toasted.

4. Drizzle the walnut mixture over the steamed green beans.

5. Season with salt and pepper.

Nutrition Per Serving

Calories: 150.5, Fat: 13.5g, Carbohydrates: 6.7g, Protein: 2.5g

Cucumber Salad With Cumin And Lemon

A light and healthy side dish.

Servings: 4

Preparation time: 15 minutes

Cooking time: 0 minutes

Ingredients:

2 English cucumbers, cut into 1/3-inch thick pieces

2 tablespoons of extra virgin olive oil

2 tablespoons of lemon juice

1/2 teaspoon of ground cumin

1/2 teaspoon of salt

1/2 teaspoon of ground pepper

Directions:

1. Add the olive oil, lemon juice, cumin and pepper to a medium-sized bowl, whisk to combine.

2. Set the cucumbers on a chopping board, cover with a paper or kitchen towel and smash the cucumbers with a mallet until it breaks.

3. Tear the mashed cucumbers with your hands and place in a colander. Season with a sprinkle of salt, combine and keep aside for 10 minutes.

4. Drain the liquid from the cucumbers by shaking the colander, transfer to a kitchen towel and pat dry.

5. Toss the dry cucumbers with the dressing.

Nutrition Per Serving

Calories: 81, Fat: 7g, Carbohydrates: 4g, Protein: 2g

Avocado Slaw

Serve with your favorite BBQ.

Servings: 4

Preparation time: 15 minutes

Cooking time: 0 minutes

Ingredients:

1 14-oz bag of precut coleslaw

1/4 cup of fresh cilantro, chopped

1/4 cup of chopped red onion

2 tablespoons of extra virgin olive oil

1 tablespoon of white vinegar

2 ripe avocados, mashed

Juice of 2 limes

1/2 teaspoon of salt

1/4 teaspoon of liquid lemon stevia

1/4 teaspoon of pepper

Directions:

1. In a large bowl, mix the onion, coleslaw and cilantro.

2. Whisk the vinegar, stevia, lime juice, olive oil, salt and pepper in a small bowl.

3. Add the avocado and stir to combine.

4. Toss the dressing with the coleslaw mixture.

5. Keep chilled for an hour before you serve.

Nutrition Per Serving

Calories: 104, Fat: 9.8g, Carbohydrates: 6.4g, Protein: 0.8g

Cabbage Salad
A healthy Mediterranean inspired dish.

Servings: 6

Preparation time: 10 minutes

Cooking time: 0 minutes

Ingredients:

3 cups of red cabbage, coarsely chopped

3 cups of green cabbage, coarsely chopped

3 tablespoons of lemon juice

1 tablespoon of olive oil

1 teaspoon of cumin

1 teaspoon of black pepper

1 teaspoon of dried mint

1/2 teaspoon of salt

1/2 teaspoon of crushed red pepper flakes

Directions:

1. Combine all the ingredients in a large bowl.

2. Chill for 1 hour at least before serving.

Nutrition Per Serving

Calories: 47, Fat: 2g, Carbohydrates: 6g, Protein: 1g

Carrot Chips

Fast and easy.

Servings: 2

Preparation time: 10 minutes

Cooking time: 14 minutes

Ingredients:

1 teaspoon of olive oil

2 carrots, peeled and cut into long flat pieces

Salt

Pepper

Directions:

1. Preheat oven to 350F and line a baking pan with parchment paper.

2. Toss the ingredients together in a large bowl and spread it out in the baking pan.

3. Place the pan on the rack closest to the source of heat and bake for 6 minutes.

4. Transfer the pan to a lower rack and bake for an extra 6-8 minutes until crisp.

Nutrition Per Serving

Calories: 45, Fat: 2g, Carbohydrates: 6g, Protein: 1g

Cauliflower Rice

A "grain" that is low carb and incredibly nutritious.

Servings: 6

Preparation time: 5 minutes

Cooking time: 10 minutes

Ingredients:

1/2 cauliflower, cut into small florets and shredded

1 cup of full fat coconut cream

1 teaspoon of cilantro

1.4 cup of unsweetened coconut, shredded

Salt

Directions:

1. Put the shredded cauliflower and the other ingredients in a large pan.

2. Cook over medium high heat until it softens.

Nutrition Per Serving

Calories: 84, Fat: 6.9g, Carbohydrates: 4.5g, Protein: 2g

Sesame Garlic Green Beans

Pair this amazing dish with anything!

Servings: 4

Preparation time: 2 minutes

Cooking time: 3 minutes

Ingredients:

1 pound of green beans

1 tablespoon of sesame seeds

1 tablespoon of sesame oil

1 clove of garlic, crushed

Directions:

1. Heat the oil in a pan and sauté the garlic until fragrant.

2. Cook the beans in the pan for 1 minute.

3. Toss the cooked green beans with the sesame seeds.

Nutrition Per Serving

Calories: 62, Fat: 2g, Carbohydrates: 9g, Protein: 3g

SOUPS

Broccoli Soup

It's warm, creamy, and rich.

Servings: 4

Preparation time: 15 minutes

Cooking time: 30 minutes

Ingredients:

1 can of full fat coconut milk

3 cups of chopped broccoli florets

3 cups of chopped celery

2 cups of vegetable broth

1/2 teaspoon of garlic pepper

1/2 teaspoon of onion powder

Red pepper flakes

Salt

Pepper

Directions:

1. In a pot, add the milk, broccoli, celery, broth, garlic pepper and onion powder. Cook for about 30 minutes over medium heat until the broccoli and celery are tender.

2. Blend the soup carefully in a blender until smooth.

Nutrition Per Serving

Calories: 200, Fat: 17g, Carbohydrates: 5g, Protein: 4g

Roasted Tomato Soup

Extremely delicious and simple to prepare.

Servings: 6

Preparation time: 10 minutes

Cooking time: 40 minutes

Ingredients:

10 medium Roma tomatoes, cut into 1-inch cubes

4 garlic cloves, crushed

1/4 cup of coconut cream

1/4 cup of water

2 tablespoons of fresh basil, minced

1 tablespoon of olive oil

1/2 teaspoon of sea salt

1/4 teaspoon of black pepper

Directions:

1. Preheat oven to 400F.

2. Use foil to line a baking pan and lightly grease it.

3. In a bowl, combine the garlic, oil and tomatoes. Toss to coat well.

4. Arrange the tomatoes on the baking pan in a single layer. Roast for about 20-25 minutes or until the tomatoes skin puckers.

5. Purée the mixture with its juices in a blender until smooth.

6. Add the processed mixture to a pot over medium heat.

7. Add the salt and pepper to season.

8. Allow to simmer for 10-15 minutes.

9. Add the basil and coconut cream; stir and serve.

Nutrition Per Serving

Calories: 95, Fat: 6g, Carbohydrates: 9g, Protein: 2g

Asparagus Soup

Bursting with tons of amazing flavors.

Servings: 4

Preparation time: 10 minutes

Cooking time: 25 minutes

Ingredients:

1 1/2 pounds of asparagus, ends removed and cut into 1-in pieces

4 cups of vegetable broth

1/2 cup of dry white wine

1/4 cup of coconut cream

3-4 fresh tarragon sprigs with extra for garnish

2 garlic cloves, minced

2 small shallots, crushed

2 tablespoons of unsalted vegan butter

Salt

Freshly ground pepper

Directions:

1. Melt the butter in a large pan over medium heat and sauté the garlic and shallots for about 3-5 minutes until aromatic and translucent. Lightly season with salt and pepper.

2. Pour in the wine and allow the liquid to reduce by about 75%.

3. Add the vegetable broth, asparagus and tarragon; allow the soup to boil.

4. Turn down the heat and simmer for about 10-15 minutes until the asparagus is soft.

5. Carefully transfer the soup to a blender or food processor and blend until smooth.

6. Pour the soup back into the pan and cook over low heat.

7. Stir in the cream slowly and adjust seasoning.

8. Garnish with chopped tarragon and serve.

Nutrition Per Serving

Calories: 94, Fat: 4.3g, Carbohydrates: 7.8g, Protein: 3.1g

Pistachio Broccoli Soup

A pleasing heartwarming soup.

Servings: 3 minutes

Preparation time: 10 minutes

Cooking time: 15 minutes

Ingredients:

1 broccoli head, cut into florets and stem chopped

2 1/2 cups of vegetable broth

1/4 cup of pistachios

3 scallions, chopped

1 clove of garlic, chopped

1 teaspoon of olive oil

Sea salt

Pepper

Directions:

1. In a pan, heat the oil over low heat and sauté the garlic and scallions for about 7 minutes until sweet and soft.

2. Add the pistachios and pour in the stock.

3. Steam the broccoli for 5 minutes.

4. Blend the broccoli and pan mixture in a food processor or blender until smooth.

5. Add salt and pepper to season.

Nutrition Per Serving

Calories: 114, Fat: 7.1g, Carbohydrates: 7g, Protein: 5.7g

Chipotle Pumpkin Soup

Best believe that you have never tasted soup this good.

Servings: 6

Preparation time: 5 minutes

Cooking time: 16 minutes

Ingredients:

32 ounces of vegetable broth

2 cups of pumpkin purée

1/2 cup of coconut cream

1/2 cup of chopped onions

2 tablespoons of olive oil

1 tablespoon of chipotles in adobo sauce

1 garlic clove, chopped

2 teaspoons of granulated sugar substitute

2 teaspoons of red wine vinegar

1 teaspoon of ground cumin

1 teaspoon of ground coriander

1/8 teaspoon of ground allspice

Salt

Pepper

Directions:

1. In a medium pan heat oil and sauté the garlic and onions for 3-4 minutes until translucent.

2. Add the cumin, chipotles, sugar substitute, coriander and allspice; cook for an additional 2 minutes.

3. Add the broth and puree; let it simmer for about 5 minutes.

4. Transfer the soup to a blender and blend until smooth.

5. Return soup to pot, add the vinegar and cream; allow to simmer for 5 minutes.

6. Season with salt and pepper.

Nutrition Per Serving

Calories: 138, Fat: 12g, Carbohydrates: 6g, Protein: 2g

Basil Zucchini Soup
Warm yourself from the inside on cold days with this hearty soup.

Servings: 4

Preparation time: 10 minutes

Cooking time: 15 minutes

Ingredients:

1 pound of zucchini, trimmed and chunked

2 cups of vegetable stock

1/2 cup of vegan whipping cream

1/3 cup of packed fresh basil leaves

2 garlic cloves

1 tablespoon of olive oil

1/2 teaspoon of pepper

1/2 teaspoon of salt

Directions:

1. In a large Dutch oven or pan heat oil until shimmering over medium heat.

2. Sauté the garlic for about 1 minute until aromatic.

3. Add the salt, pepper and zucchini; cook for about 4-5 minutes until it is just tender.

4. Pour in the stock, stir and allow to boil. Turn down the heat and allow to simmer for 10 minutes.

5. Remove from heat, add the basil and allow it wilt for some minutes.

6. Blend the soup in a food processor or blender.

7. Return the soup to pan and add the cream. Adjust seasoning if desired.

Nutrition Per Serving

Calories: 164, Fat: 13.96g, Carbohydrates: 5.83g, Protein: 3.86g

Zoodle Soup

Prepared with ingredients grown in your backyard.

Servings: 2

Preparation time: 5 minutes

Cooking time: 8 minutes

Ingredients:

2 large garden tomatoes, chopped

2 basil leaves

1 garlic clove, crushed

1 medium zucchini, spiralized

1 teaspoon of olive oil

Directions:

1. In a pan heat oil and sauté the zucchini and garlic for 3-4 minutes.

2. Add the tomatoes along with its juices and cook for an additional 3-4 minutes.

3. Garnish with basil and serve.

Nutrition Per Serving

Calories: 60, Fat: 2.8g, Carbohydrates: 8.6g, Protein: 2.4g

Miso Soup

A tasty Asian delicacy.

Servings: 4

Preparation time: 15 minutes

Cooking time: 50 minutes

Ingredients:

3 cups of water

3 cups of vegetable stock

2 cups of sliced mushrooms

1 cup of carrot, julienned

3 garlic cloves, crushed

3 scallions thinly sliced

1 large handful of baby spinach

2 tbsp miso paste, thin with small water

1 tbsp tamari or amino acid

1 tbsp extra virgin olive oil

1 tbsp sesame seed oil, toasted

1/2 teaspoon of fresh ginger root, grated

A pinch of wakame flakes

Directions:

1. Heat olive oil over medium low heat in a large pot and saute the ginger root and garlic until fragrant.

2. Add the mushrooms and cook until it releases its moisture.

3. Pour in the water and broth; leave to simmer for 30-45 minutes on low.

4. Remove from heat, add the tamari, miso paste and sesame oil.

5. Add the wakame flakes and carrots to a serving bowl, ladle the miso broth over it and garnish with the scallions.

Nutrition Per Serving

Calories: 84, Fat: 5.7g, Carbohydrates: 5.7g, Protein: 3.5g

Asparagus Hazelnut Soup

A great cold reliever.

Servings: 4

Preparation time: 20 minutes

Cooking time: 15 minutes

Ingredients:

2 1/2 cups of fresh asparagus, cut and trimmed

2 cups of vegetable stock

1/2 cup of unsweetened almond milk

1/2 cup of sweet onion, chopped

1/3 cup of toasted whole hazelnuts

3 cloves of garlic, diced

2 tablespoons of lemon juice

2 tablespoons of fresh basil, chopped

1 tablespoon of olive oil

2 teaspoons of low sodium soy sauce

1/4 teaspoon of salt

A dash of crushed red pepper flakes

Shaved asparagus, optional

Directions:

1. Heat the olive oil in a large pan over medium heat and sauté the garlic, pepper flakes and onion for 4-5 minutes until the onion is tender.

2. Add the stock and asparagus; leave to boil.

3. Lower the heat, simmer for 6-8 minutes while covered until the asparagus is soft. Remove pan from heat and allow to cool a bit.

4. Blend the basil, lemon juice and hazelnuts in a blender.

5. Add the cooked asparagus to the blender and purée until it is creamy and smooth.

6. Return the pureed mixture to the pan and add the milk, salt and soy sauce.

7. Stir the soup but do not allow it boil.

8. Garnish with the shaved asparagus and serve.

Nutrition Per Serving

Calories: 164, Fat: 13g, Carbohydrates: 7g, Protein: 5g

Creamy Broccoli And Coconut Soup
Boost your immunity with this nutrient-dense soup.

Servings: 4

Preparation time: 10 minutes

Cooking time: 27 minutes

Ingredients:

4 cups of vegetable broth

3/4 cup of full fat coconut milk

1 head of broccoli, cut into florets

2 shallots, peeled and chopped

2 garlic cloves, peeled and minced

2 tablespoons of virgin coconut oil, divided

2 tablespoons of coconut cream

1/3 teaspoon of salt

1/4 teaspoon of cracked black pepper

A handful of watercress, optional

Directions:

1. In a saucepan, simmer the vegetable broth for 20 minutes over medium heat until half of the broth is absorbed.

2. In another pan, heat a tablespoon of oil over medium heat and sauté the onion for 2 minutes.

3. Add the garlic and sauté for an extra minute. Remove from heat.

4. When the vegetable broth is reduced, add the broccoli florets and bring down from heat. Leave to sit for 10 minutes.

5. Return saucepan to heat; add the sautéed vegetables, milk, salt and pepper. Stir and heat for 1-2 minutes.

6. Transfer the soup to a blender, add the cream, watercress and remaining coconut oil. Blend until smooth.

7. Return soup to saucepan and heat.

Nutrition Per Serving

Calories: 311, Fat: 29.5g, Carbohydrates: 8g, Protein: 4.8g

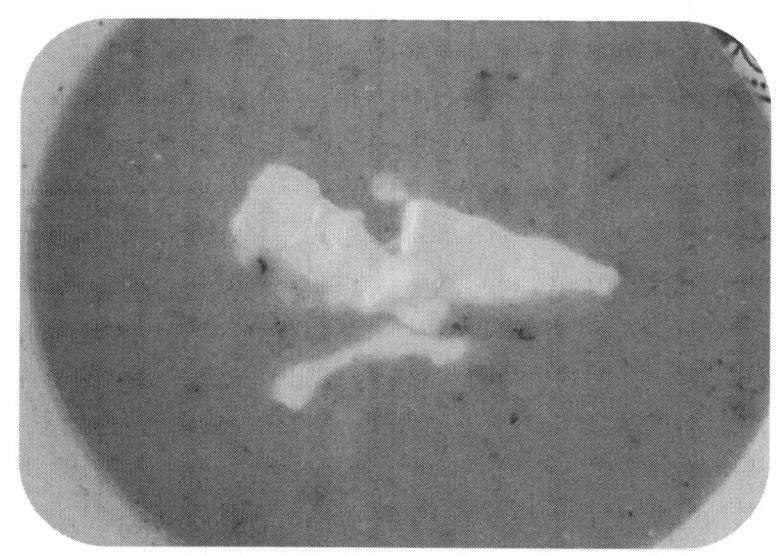

Broccoli Soup

Cremini Mushroom Soup
It is rich and packed with aromatic flavors.

Servings: 6

Preparation time: 10 minutes

Cooking time: 17 minutes

Ingredients:

1 1/2 pounds of cremini mushrooms, chopped

4 cups of low sodium vegetable stock

1/2 cup of chopped onions

1/4 cup of fresh flat leaf parsley, chopped

1 tablespoon of olive oil

1 garlic clove, crushed

1/2 teaspoon of black pepper

Salt

Directions:

1. Heat oil in a medium pot and sauté the garlic and onions until it is translucent.

2. Add the mushrooms, stock, salt, parsley and pepper. Cook for about 15 minutes at a gentle boil until the cremini mushrooms wilts.

3. Season with salt.

Nutrition Per Serving

Calories: 71, Fat: 3g, Carbohydrates: 8g, Protein: 4g

Creamy Green Soup
A healthy bowl of nourishing goodness.

Servings: 4

Preparation time: 5 minutes

Cooking time: 0 minutes

Ingredients:

2 cups of spinach leaves

1/4 cup of vegetable stock

1/2 cup of English cucumbers

1/2 cup of red bell peppers

1 garlic clove

1 avocado

1 green onion

1 tablespoon of lemon juice

1 tablespoon of soy seasoning

Freshly ground pepper

A pinch of chili powder, optional

Directions:

Blend all the ingredients together in a blender until smooth and creamy.

Nutrition Per Serving

Calories: 95, Fat: 7.6g, Carbohydrates: 6.7g, Protein: 2.1g

Roasted Garlic Soup
This has just the right amount of aromatic flavors.

Servings: 6

Preparation time: 10 minutes

Cooking time: 1 hour

Ingredients:

6 cups of vegetable stock

1 large head of cauliflower, chopped

3 shallots, chopped

2 garlic bulbs, peeled

1 tablespoon of extra virgin olive oil

3/4 teaspoon of sea salt

Freshly ground pepper

Directions:

1. Preheat oven to 400F.

2. Chop off about 1/4-in from the top of the peeled garlic, set it on a piece of aluminum foil and coat each of the garlic with 1/ teaspoon of oil.

3. Roast for 35 minutes. Leave to cool a bit, remove the foil and squeeze out the garlic from its cloves.

4. In the meantime, heat the remaining oil in a medium pan and sauté the shallots for about 6 minutes until it is soft and starts to brown.

5. Add the garlic and the rest of the ingredients, cover and allow to boil.

6. Lower heat to low and simmer the soup until the cauliflower is soft, for 15-20 minutes.

7. Transfer soup to blender or food processor and process for about 30 seconds until smooth.

8. Adjust seasoning if desired.

Nutrition Per Serving

Calories: 73, Fat: 2.4g, Carbohydrates: 9.2g, Protein: 2.1g

Basil Tomato Soup

A spicy soup perfect for winter.

Servings: 6

Preparation time: 10 minutes

Cooking time: 50 minutes

Ingredients:

3 pounds of plum tomatoes, divided

1 quart of vegetable broth

6 garlic cloves, minced

1 sweet onion, chopped

1/2 cup of basil, roughly chopped

3 tablespoons of olive oil, divided

2 tablespoons of tomato paste

2 tablespoons of vegan butter

1 tablespoon of sriracha

1 tablespoon of salt

1 teaspoon of crushed red pepper

1/2 teaspoon of thyme

1/2 teaspoon of pepper

1/2 teaspoon of cayenne

1/2 teaspoon of paprika

Directions:

1. Wash and thoroughly dry 2/3 of the tomatoes, about 8, cut in half lengthwise and place on a greased cookie sheet with the cut side facing up. Chop the remaining tomatoes into small pieces.

2. Sprinkle salt and oil over the tomatoes and roast in the oven for about 40 minutes at 400F until wrinkly but dark.

3. Meanwhile, heat a tablespoon of oil in a large pot and sauté the garlic and onion until translucent and fragrant.

4. Add the chopped tomatoes and broth, bring to a boil.

5. Add the basil leaves, butter, tomato paste and spices while cooking over medium heat.

6. Add the roasted tomatoes at this point, reduce heat to low and give it time to simmer for about 40 minutes.

7. Blend the soup in a blender until smooth.

Nutrition Per Serving

Calories: 164, Fat: 12g, Carbohydrates: 9g, Protein: 3g

Leek And Onion Soup

Warm yourself from the inside out with this filling soup.

Servings: 3

Preparation time: 10 minutes

Cooking time: 50 minutes

Ingredients:

2 cups of vegetable broth

1/4 cup of white wine

1 cup of water

2 tablespoons of olive oil

1 bay leaf

1 leek, white and green parts only, cleaned and thinly sliced

1 medium onion, thinly sliced

1 teaspoon of dried thyme

1 teaspoon of maple syrup

Salt

Pepper

Directions:

1. Heat oil in a pan and sauté the onion until translucent.

2. Add the maple syrup and leek, cook for about 30 minutes over low medium heat.

3. Pour in the broth, wine, water, thyme and bay leaf. Simmer soup for 20 minutes and discard the bay leaf.

4. Season with salt and pepper.

Nutrition Per Serving

Calories: 167.1, Fat: 10.4g, Carbohydrates: 9g, Protein: 5.1g

Yellow Squash Soup
It is rich and mouthwatering.

Servings: 8

Preparation time: 15 minutes

Cooking time: 15 minutes

Ingredients:

6 medium yellow squash, seeded and cut into cubes

6 cloves of garlic, crushed

4 fresh sprigs of thyme

2 large sweet onions, chopped

1 medium leek, white parts only, chopped

4 cups of low sodium vegetable broth

2 tablespoons of lemon juice

2 tablespoons of olive oil

1/4 teaspoon of salt

1/8 teaspoon of hot pepper sauce

Directions:

1. Heat oil in a pan and sauté the leek and onion until soft.

2. Add the garlic and cook for an extra minute.

3. Add the squash and cook for 5 minutes.

4. Add the thyme, broth and salt; allow to boil.

5. Lower heat, cover and simmer until squash is tender, for 15-20 minutes.

6. Remove the thyme and allow soup to cool a bit.

7. Blend the soup in a blender until smooth.

8. Return soup to pan, add the hot pepper sauce and lemon juice. Stir and heat through.

Nutrition Per Serving

Calories: 90, Fat: 4g, Carbohydrates: 9g, Protein: 4g

APPETIZERS

Garlic And Basil Soup

Whip up your appetite with this creamy entrée.

Servings: 4

Preparation time: 10 minutes

Cooking time: 35 minutes

Ingredients:

1 pound of red bell peppers, halved, seeded and chopped

1 big bunch of fresh basil, chopped

1 cup of cashew cream

5 cloves of garlic, peeled and sliced

1 teaspoon of Himalayan or unrefined sea salt

Directions:

1. Add all the ingredients to a large pan, stir and allow to boil.

2. Cover and leave to simmer for 30 minutes over medium low heat or until the vegetables are soft.

3. Pour into a blender and process until smooth.

Nutrition Per Serving

Calories: 228, Fat: 21.5g, Carbohydrates: 6.5g, Protein: 2.2g

Roasted Herbed Olives

A yummy Mediterranean appetizer

Servings: 8

Preparation time: 10 minutes

Cooking time: 25 minutes

Ingredients:

1 cup of kalamata olives, pitted

1 cup of black olives, pitted

1 cup of green olives, stuffed with almonds, garlic or pimento

1/4 cup of olive oil

1 tablespoon of Herbes de Provence

8-10 whole cloves of garlic, peeled

Directions:

1. Preheat oven to 425F.

2. Drain the olives and add to a small baking pan.

3. Add the Herbes de Provence, olive oil and garlic to the pan. Toss to combine.

4. Bake for 20-25 minutes or until the garlic begins to brown and the olives are sizzling. Stir the mixture after 10 minutes while baking.

5. Remove from oven and keep warm.

6. Put the warned olives in a bowl; toss with lemon zest and black pepper.

7. Garnish with rosemary or thyme if needed.

Nutrition Per Serving

Calories: 103, Fat: 10.5g, Carbohydrates: 1.8g, Protein: 0.5g

Zucchini Chips

A flavorful and bite-sized snack.

Servings:2

Preparation time: 5 minutes

Cooking time: 45 minutes

Ingredients:

1 medium-sized zucchini, cut crosswise into 1/4-inch slices

2 teaspoons of olive oil, divided

1/2 teaspoon of salt

1/4 teaspoon of ground pepper

1 teaspoon of smoked paprika

Directions:

1. Preheat oven to 250F.

2. Use parchment paper to line a baking pan and brush the paper with a teaspoon of olive oil.

3. Layer the zucchini slices into a sieve or colander and sprinkle salt on each layer. Keep aside to drain for an hour.

4. Use a paper towel to pat the zucchini dry, add the zucchini to baking pan.

5. Brush the top of the zucchini slices with the rest of the oil; sprinkle the pepper and paprika over it.

6. Bake for 45 minutes, switch off the oven and leave the chips inside for about an hour until crisp.

Nutrition Per Serving

Calories: 46, Fat: 4.68g, Carbohydrates: 1.33g, Protein: 0.42g

Energy Balls

Delicious enough to also be used as a dessert.

Servings: 15

Preparation time: 10 minutes

Cooking time: 0 minutes

Ingredients:

3 medjool dates, pit removed

1 cup of old-fashioned oats

1/4 cup of ground flaxseed

1/2 cup of almond butter

2 tablespoons of dried fruit

1 tablespoon of maple syrup

1/2 teaspoon of cinnamon

Directions:

1. In a food processor, mix the dates, maple syrup and butter until everything is mixed and the dates are well chopped.

2. Mix the remaining ingredients in a bowl and add the date mixture. Combine thoroughly.

3. Roll the mixture into 1-inch balls, put in an airtight container and keep refrigerated.

Nutrition Per Serving

Calories: 96, Fat: 6g, Carbohydrates: 9g, Protein: 2g

Marinated Mushrooms

Entertains the mouth quite well.

Servings: 4

Preparation time: 15 minutes

Cooking time: 5 minutes

Ingredients:

1 pound of cremini mushrooms

2 garlic cloves, crushed

1/4 cup of red onion, chopped

1/4 cup of white wine vinegar

1/4 cup of olive oil

2 tablespoons of fresh parsley leaves, chopped

2 teaspoons of packed brown sugar

1 bay leaf

1/2 teaspoon of whole black peppercorns

1/2 teaspoon of dried oregano

1/4 teaspoon of crushed red pepper flakes

Freshly ground black pepper

Kosher salt

Directions:

1. Bring a large pot of salted water to boil and add the mushrooms. Cook for about 3-4 minutes until it is just soft. Drain.

2. Mix the mushrooms with the peppercorns, garlic, olive oil, onion, pepper flakes, sugar, bay leaf, vinegar and oregano in a bowl. Add salt and pepper to season.

3. Put in an airtight container and refrigerate for 8 hours at least or up to 5 days.

4. Garnish with parsley and serve at room temperature.

Nutrition Per Serving

Calories: 164.6, Fat: 13.8g, Carbohydrates: 8.9g, Protein: 3.1g

Vegan Mini Quesadilla

A fun snack for the whole family.

Servings: 12

Preparation time: 10 minutes

Cooking time: 8 minutes

Ingredients:

1 1/2 ounces of vegan queso fresco, crumbled

1/4 cup of hummus

1 tablespoon of minced cilantro

1/4 teaspoon of ground cumin

1/2 California avocado, cut into 12 slices

4 whole wheat tortillas

Directions:

1. Cut 3 circles from each tortilla with a 2 1/2-inch circle cookie cutter.

2. Combine the cumin, hummus and cilantro in a small bowl. Spread a teaspoon of this mix on each of the cut tortillas.

3. Evenly divide the queso fresco and slices of avocado between the tortillas. Arrange the mixture on half of the cut tortillas.

4. Heat a pan over medium heat and cook the tortillas for 2-3 minutes on each side until they are golden brown.

Nutrition Per Serving

Calories: 66.3, Fat: 3.6g, Carbohydrates: 6.8g, Protein: 2.2g

Carrot Granola Balls

A healthy excuse to snack.

Servings: 22

Preparation time: 15 minutes

Cooking time: 0 minutes

Ingredients:

1 1/2 cups of old-fashioned oats

1/3 cup of raisins

1/3 cups of raw pecans, chopped

3/4 cup of almond butter

3/4 cup of packed carrot, grated

3 tablespoons of agave nectar

1 tablespoon of ground flaxseed

1/4 teaspoon of ground cinnamon

Directions:

1. Combine the pecans, flaxseed and oats in a large bowl.

2. Add the butter, cinnamon and agave nectar, stir to combine.

3. Add the raisins and carrots, stir thoroughly.

4. Scoop 2 tablespoons of the batter and roll into bite-sized balls.

5. Set the balls on a baking pan, cover and keep in refrigerator for an hour.

Nutrition Per Serving

Calories: 102, Fat: 6g, Carbohydrates: 10g, Protein: 3g

Parsnip Chips

A crunchy and delicious treat.

Servings: 6

Preparation time: 10 minutes

Cooking time: 35 minutes

Ingredients:

2 cups of parsnips, thinly sliced

2 teaspoons of sea salt

3 tablespoons of olive or avocado oil

Directions:

1. Preheat oven to 425F.

2. Line a baking pan with parchment paper.

3. Toss all the ingredients in a large bowl to coat and place in the prepared baking pan.

4. Bake for 25-35 minutes or until it is crisp and brown.

Nutrition Per Serving

Calories: 85, Fat: 6g, Carbohydrates: 8g, Protein: 1g

Buffalo Cauliflower Wings

A much healthier version of the classic American recipe.

Servings: 8

Preparation time: 10 minutes

Cooking time: 30 minutes

Ingredients:

For the sauce:

4 tablespoons of hot sauce

2 garlic cloves, minced

2 tablespoons of coconut oil

A pinch of sea salt

For the wings:

4 cups of cauliflower florets, cut into bite-sized pieces

1/2 cup of filtered water

1/2 cup of cassava flour

1 tablespoon of hot sauce

2 teaspoons of seasoned salt

Directions:

1. Heat all the sauce ingredients in a small pot.

2. Preheat oven to 450F.

3. Use parchment paper to line a baking pan.

4. In a bowl, mix the flour and salt thoroughly. Keep aside.

5. In another bowl, mix the hot sauce and water. Combine this mixture with the flour mixture.

6. Coat the florets in the batter mixture and place on the baking pan.

7. Put pan in the middle rack and bake for 25-30 minutes until crisp.

8. Drizzle baked florets with the sauce and serve.

Nutrition Per Serving

Calories: 65, Fat: 3g, Carbohydrates: 8g, Protein: 1g

Cabbage Chips

A dish that readily whets the appetite.

Servings: 4

Preparation time: 5 minutes

Cooking time: 3 hours 2 minutes

Ingredients:

1 head of cabbage, cored and leaves separated

Celtic sea salt

Directions:

1. Preheat oven to 200F.

2. Boil the cabbage leaves in salty water for about 2 minutes until translucent.

3. Transfer the leaves immediately to a large bowl containing ice water, with a slotted spoon. Allow to cool, drain and dry well.

4. Place a wire rack in a rimmed baking pan and arrange the leaves on it in an even layer.

5. Bake for about 3 hours until it is crispy and totally dry.

6. Season with the sea salt.

Nutrition Per Serving

Calories: 40, Fat: 0g, Carbohydrates: 5g, Protein: 3g

Oat Peanut Butter Energy Balls

Great for pre-workout and after workout snacking.

Servings: 12

Preparation time: 15 minutes

Cooking time: 0 minutes

Ingredients:

1/2 cup of rolled oats

1/4 cup of peanut butter

3/4 cup of medjool dates, chopped

Chia seeds

Directions:

1. In a small bowl, soak the dates for 5-10 minutes in hot water. Drain.

2. Process the dates, peanut butter and oats in a food processor until they are chopped finely.

3. Roll the mixture into balls.

4. Garnish the balls with the chia seeds if using.

Nutrition Per Serving

Calories: 73, Fat: 3g, Carbohydrates: 10g, Protein: 2g

Roasted Sesame Seeds And Edamame

This delicious snack packs a burst of energy.

Servings: 4

Preparation time: 5 minutes

Cooking time: 20 minutes

Ingredients:

2 cups of frozen edamame, shelled and thawed

1 tablespoon of black sesame seeds

2 teaspoons of olive oil

1 teaspoon of sea salt

Directions:

1. Preheat oven to 450F.

2. Toss the edamame and salt in a bowl. Add the salt to season.

3. Place the edamame in a baking pan and bake for 12-15 minutes.

4. Remove the pan from the oven and sprinkle the sesame seeds over it.

5. Bake again for 5 minutes.

Nutrition Per Serving

Calories: 153, Fat: 8.3g, Carbohydrates: 5.2g, Protein: 13.4g

Peanut Butter Balls

A delicious snack to keep your mouth busy.

Servings: 16

Preparation time: 15 minutes

Cooking time: 0 minutes

Ingredients:

1/2 cup of peanut butter

1/3 cup of rolled oats

1/4 cup of apple cider

1/4 cup of brown rice crisp cereal

1/4 cup of unsweetened coconut flakes

1/4 cup of whole quick oats

1/4 cup of wheat germ

1 tablespoon of maple syrup

1/2 teaspoon of ground cinnamon

Directions:

1. In a bowl, combine all the ingredients except the cereal.

2. Roll the mixture into balls whose diameters are 1-inch.

3. Put the cereal in a shallow plate and dredge the balls in it.

Nutrition Per Serving

Calories: 79, Fat: 4.8g, Carbohydrates: 6.3g, Protein: 3.5g

Pickled Turnips
Simply irresistible!

Servings: 8

Preparation time: 5 minutes

Cooking time: 2 minutes

Ingredients:

1.1 pounds of white turnips, peeled and cut into 1/4-inch sticks

1 1/2 cups of water, divided

2/3 cup of white vinegar

2 garlic cloves, peeled and minced

1 small-sized beet, peeled and cut into 1/4-inch sticks

2 tablespoons of coarse sea salt

Directions:

1. Divide the water into half. Add the salt to one half, cook and stir until it dissolves. Allow to cool to room temperature.

2. In a large pickling jar, add half of the beet, turnips and garlic. Repeat this process until you add all the vegetables to the jar..

3. Pour in the salted water and the remaining water.

4. Pour in the vinegar and close the lid tightly.

5. Refrigerate for 5 days at least before serving.

Nutrition Per Serving

Calories: 18, Fat: 0.06g, Carbohydrates: 4.02g, Protein: 0.56g

DESSERTS

Coconut Chocolate Fat Bombs

A healthy way to satisfy your sweet tooth.

Servings: 10-12

Preparation time:

Cooking time: 5 minutes

Ingredients:

1 cup of canned full fat coconut milk

1 cup of coconut butter

1 cup of shredded coconut

4 tablespoons of cocoa powder

1 teaspoon of vanilla extract

1 teaspoon of stevia powder extract

3-4 drops of essential peppermint oil

Directions:

1. Put a few inches of water in a saucepan and set a glass bowl over it so as to form a double boiler.

2. Mix the milk, butter, cocoa powder, vanilla extract, stevia and peppermint oil in a double boiler and cook over medium heat.

3. Remove from heat when the ingredients are well mixed.

4. Refrigerate the bowl for about 30 minutes or until the mixture is hard enough to form balls.

5. Roll the mixture into balls of 1-inch and dredge in the shredded coconut.

6. Put in a plate and keep in the refrigerator for an hour

Nutrition Per Serving

Calories: 251, Fat: 21.7g, Carbohydrates: 8.4g, Protein: 2.8g

Matcha Mint Fat Bombs

They are sooo good!

Servings: 10

Preparation time: 10 minutes

Cooking time: 0 minutes

Ingredients:

1/2 cup of coconut oil

3/4 cup of hemp seeds

2 tablespoons of coconut butter, melted

1 teaspoon of matcha powder

1/2 teaspoon of mint extract

1/2 teaspoon of vanilla extract

Liquid stevia

Directions:

1. Combine all the ingredients except the coconut butter in a blender, then process until smooth (you need a high-power blender). Pour the mixture into a silicon muffin pan.

2. Drizzle the melted butter on top of the muffin cups.

Nutrition Per Serving

Calories: 199.6, Fat: 20.2g, Carbohydrates: 1.1g, Protein: 4.2g

Pumpkin Spice Muffins
Refreshing and delicious.

Servings: 12

Preparation time: 15 minutes

Cooking time: 45 minutes

Ingredients:

1 cup of canned pumpkin

1/4 cup of granulated sugar substitute

1/4 cup of non dairy milk

1/4 cup of peanut butter

1/4 cup of ground flaxseed

6 tablespoons of coconut flour

2 tablespoons of pumpkin spice mix

1 tablespoon of baking powder

Directions:

1. Preheat oven to 350F and line a muffin tin with parchment paper.

2. Mix the butter, pumpkin, sweetener, flaxseed and milk in a bowl until well combined.

3. Mix the flour, baking powder and spices in another bowl.

4. Add the dry ingredients to the wet ingredients and combine thoroughly until the flour is well mixed. Leave to stand for some minutes to allow the flour absorb the moisture.

5. Evenly divide the mixture into the muffin tin.

6. Bake for 45 minutes.

Nutrition Per Serving

Calories: 72, Fat: 4.7g, Carbohydrates: 2.6g, Protein: 2.7g

Dark Chocolate Caramels

Sinfully decadent.

Servings: 24

Preparation time: 25 minutes

Cooking time: 0 minutes

Ingredients:

2 cups of pitted medjool dates

1 1/2 cups of unsalted roasted sunflower seeds

3/4 cup of nondairy chocolate chips

1/4 teaspoon of fine sea salt

Sea salt

Directions:

1. Blend the fine sea salt, dates and sunflower seeds in a food processor until it forms a thick batter.

2. Put the batter into an 8x8-inch baking pan and press down firmly. Freeze pan for 20 minutes at least.

3. Meanwhile melt the chocolate chips in a double boiler.

4. Remove the frozen pan and loosen its edges with a butter knife. Line a cutting board with parchment paper, turn the pan over the board and divide the date mixture into small pieces.

5. Drizzle a small dollop of chocolate with a spoon on the top of each pieces. Get the melted chocolate along its edges and also smooth it out with the spoon's back.

6. Sprinkle the sea salt over it and refrigerate for 20 minutes in order to make the chocolate hard.

Nutrition Per Serving

Calories: 60, Fat: 2.9g, Carbohydrates: 8.4g, Protein: 1.2g

Blueberry Cobbler

A sweet treat that is magical for your cravings.

Servings: 9

Preparation time: 15 minutes

Cooking time: 22 minutes

Ingredients:

Filling:

3 cups of blueberries

2 tablespoons of swerve

1/4 teaspoon of xanthan gum

1 teaspoon of lemon juice

Toppings:

2/3 cup of almond flour

2 tablespoons of almond butter

2 tablespoons of swerve

1/2 teaspoon of lemon zest

Directions:

1. Combine all the filling ingredients in a medium bowl until the berries are well coated. Pour this mixture into a 9x9 baking pan.

2. Put the butter in a bowl or coffee mug and melt in the microwave.

3. Add the remaining topping ingredients and stir to form a crumbly batter.

4. Break this batter into pea-sized lumps over the blueberries with your hands.

5. Bake in the oven for 22 minutes at 375F until the blueberries are bubbly and the crust turns golden brown.

Nutrition Per Serving

Calories: 95, Fat: 6g, Carbohydrates: 6.5, Protein: 2g

Tiger Butter Candies
These candies couldn't be easier to whip up.

Servings: 16

Preparation time: 15 minutes

Cooking time: 0 minutes

Ingredients:

4 ounces of coconut butter

4 ounces of no-sugar dark chocolate

4 ounces of cocoa butter

1/2 cup of creamy along or peanut butter

1/4 cup of powdered swerve

1/2 teaspoon of vanilla extract

1/8 teaspoon of xanthan gum

Directions:

1. Use parchment paper to line a square baking sheet.

2. Melt the butters and swerve in a medium pan over medium low heat.

3. Add the xanthan gum and vanilla extract. Whisk until it is well combined.

4. Pour the mixture into the baking sheet and spread it out to the edges.

5. Keep it in the refrigerator for 10-15 minutes to harden it.

6. Over a pan of nearly simmering water, place a heatproof bowl to form a double boiler and melt the chocolate chips until smooth. Stir while it is melting.

7. Finally, drizzle the chocolate over the baking sheet mixture and use a knife to swirl it gently.

8. Keep in the refrigerator to harden and then divide into bars.

Nutrition Per Serving

Calories: 187, Fat: 17.30g, Carbohydrates: 5.90g, Protein: 3.04g

Brownies

It's dairy-free and sugar-free.

Servings: 32

Preparation time: 15 minutes

Cooking time: 0 minutes

Ingredients:

8 pitted dates

1 ripe banana

2 cups of rolled oats

1 cup of raw cashew

1/3 cup of unsweetened cocoa powder

1/4 cup of walnuts, chopped

1/4 cup of applesauce

1/4 teaspoon of salt

Directions:

1. Blend the cashew, oats, cocoa powder, dates and salt in a food processor until it forms a smooth flour.

2. Add the applesauce and banana, blend to form a thick batter that is slightly sticky.

3. Lightly grease a 7x11 baking pan with cooking spray.

4. Pour the batter into the prepared pan and use a spatula to press it down firmly.

5. Add the walnuts and also press it into the batter.

6. Refrigerate for 1 hour at least to harden.

7. Remove from fridge and cut into 32 bars.

Nutrition Per Serving

Calories: 59, Fat: 2.7g, Carbohydrates: 8.0g, Protein: 1.7g

Chocolate Cake

No one will be able to resist this delicious treat.

Servings: 12

Preparation time: 10 minutes

Cooking time: 30 minutes

Ingredients:

1 cup of sesame meal or flour

1 cup of swerve

1 cup of water

1/2 cup of ground flaxseed

1/3 cup of unsweetened cocoa powder

5 tablespoons of sunflower oil

1 teaspoon of baking powder

1 teaspoon of white vinegar

1 teaspoon of baking soda

1 teaspoon of pure vanilla extract

1/2 teaspoon of chocolate liquid stevia

1/2 teaspoon of salt

Directions:

1. Preheat oven to 350F and line a 8x8 baking sheet with parchment paper.

2. In a bowl, whisk the flour, flaxseed, cocoa powder, swerve, baking powder, baking soda and salt together. Create 1 large depression and 2 small depressions in the batter.

3. Pour the sunflower oil into the large depression, stevia into a small depression and vinegar into the second small depression.

4. Add water and stir until it is smooth.

5. Put the mixture into the prepared baking sheet and spread it out.

6. Put the sheet into the middle rack of the oven.

7. Bake the batter for 30 minutes or until a toothpick inserted in its center comes out clean.

8. Cool for 10 minutes, hold the ends of the parchment paper and remove the cake.

9. Slice the cake on a cutting board.

Nutrition Per Serving

Calories: 167, Fat: 14.3g, Carbohydrates: 7.2g, Protein: 6.8g

Vegan Truffles

Devour this treat without feeling guilty.

Servings: 12

Preparation time: 15 minutes

Cooking time: 0 minutes

Ingredients:

3 tablespoons of coconut butter

2 tablespoons of coconut oil

2 tablespoons of unsweetened cocoa powder

2 tablespoons of almond butter

1 tablespoon of cacao nibs

2 teaspoons of mint extract

1 teaspoon of maple syrup

1/4 teaspoon of pure vanilla extract

Directions:

1. In a bowl, combine the oil, butters, and vanilla until smooth.

2. Add the nibs, mint extract, maple syrup, and vanilla extract. Combine well.

3. Harden the batter for about 10 minutes in the freezer.

4. Remove from the freezer and use your hands to roll the batter into 1-inch balls.

5. Coat the balls in the cocoa powder and place on a dish.

6. Keep in the refrigerator to harden.

7. Serve the truffles chilled.

Nutrition Per Serving

Calories: 69, Fat: 6.5g, Carbohydrates: 2.9g, Protein: 1.2g

Chocolate Chip Pumpkin Cookie
Deliciously chewy and decadent.

Servings: 12

Preparation time: 10 minutes

Cooking time: 25 minutes

Ingredients:

1/2 cup of unsweetened almond butter

1/4 cup of granulated erythriol

1/4 cup of unsweetened pumpkin purée

2 tablespoons of chocolate chips

1 tablespoon of coconut flour

1 teaspoon of cinnamon

1/2 teaspoon of baking powder

1/4 teaspoon of nutmeg

1/4 teaspoon of ground cloves

/4 teaspoon of stevia powder

1/4 teaspoon of ginger powder

1/4 teaspoon of cardamom powder

Directions:

1. Preheat oven to 350F and line 1 or 2 baking pans with parchment paper.

2. Using a hand mixer, combine all the ingredients in a bowl.

3. Scoop the dough with an ice cream scoop and place in the baking pans. Slightly flatten them with a fork in order to shape into cookies.

4. Bake for 25 minutes.

Nutrition Per Serving

Calories: 88, Fat: 7.5g, Carbohydrates: 4.74g, Protein: 3.74g

Almond Chocolate Smoothie

Another excuse to enjoy your chocolate.

Servings: 1

Preparation time: 5 minutes

Cooking time: 0 minutes

Ingredients:

8 raw almonds

1 cup of unsweetened almond milk

3 ice cubes

1/2 scoop of chocolate protein powder

Directions:

Blend ingredients in a blender until smooth.

Nutrition Per Serving

Calories: 153, Fat: 7.7g, Carbohydrates: 6.2g, Protein: 15.6g

The End

Made in the USA
Middletown, DE
09 August 2018